Armed Struggle in Africa

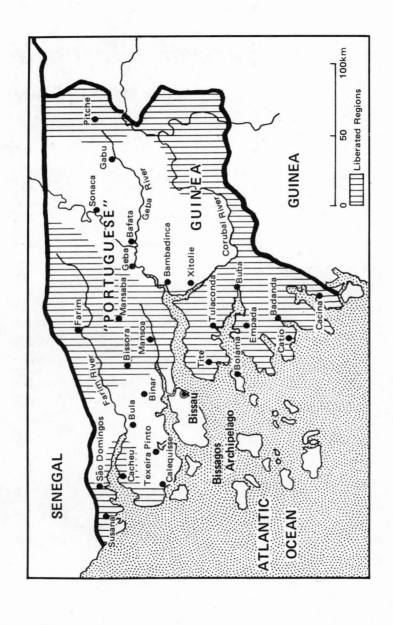

Armed Struggle in Africa

With the Guerrillas in "Portuguese" Guinea

by Gérard Chaliand

Introduction by
Basil Davidson

Translated by David Rattray
and Robert Leonhardt

 New York and London

To the memory of my father

Contents

Introduction
by Basil Davidson

"There is no new entity born of colonialism," wrote Frantz Fanon back in 1958; and everything that has happened since then seems to have confirmed this. Many peoples today need a renewal of their civilization, but none so obviously and urgently as the colonized peoples. Whatever colonialism, imperialism, capitalism may or may not have achieved, one thing is certain about them. They have utterly failed to raise those structures—whether social or moral, political or economic—upon which the deprived peoples, the abused peoples, the "underdeveloped" peoples as they are sometimes if odiously called, can carry themselves into a new civilization capable of standing and evolving on its own foundations.

Nowhere is this more plainly true than in the Portuguese colonies. Forty years of Salazarist rule, of clerico-fascist stagnation and strangulation, have most desperately mocked the "civilizing mission" that was once so often advanced as the justification for Europe's "African trusteeship." Not only no schools except for the favored few—the favored one half of one per cent of "the natives"—not only no social services in any way commensurate with the scientific and financial possibilities of the twentieth century, and no democratic institutions of any kind. Not only all that, but, beyond all that, no scope for self-respect, for decent hope in life's possibly becoming better, for even the most minimal participation in the tides and movements, triumphs, aspirations of the rest of mankind. Truly, from these aspects the position of the colonized peoples of Portugal may be said, in some words of Amilcar Cabral's eight years ago, to be absurd.

Absurd, but not mysterious, not accidental. Colonies have not

ix

been for nothing. Portuguese colonies have proved handsomely profitable to the large trading companies whose boards of directors have been filled with the beneficiaries of Salazar's "New State." These colonies have provided closed markets for Portuguese exports such as textiles, wine, and manpower for whom there were no jobs at home. They have brought in useful "colonial products" such as cotton and groundnuts, cultivated by forced or semi-forced labor paid at the cheapest price. They have fed the imperialist nostalgia of a regime whose ideas and myths were rooted in the Middle Ages.

Absurd, but also not defeated, not tragic. Gérard Chaliand's vivid little book tells the story of how a handful of brave men and women took their fate in their own hands, and, against bitter odds, prepared and led a people's struggle for the new civilization that they need. This African epic is one of courage; but it is also one of success. Nothing is more remarkable in Chaliand's pages than the portrayal of the awakening consciousness of ordinary men and women, of their understanding of the need to accept any and every personal sacrifice in order to change not only their own lives, but the lives of their whole people. Nothing is more heartening than the progress that he shows them as having made.

In these last few years, as Chaliand now reminds us, not far short of forty percent of the Portuguese budget had to be spent on "defense," while the period of obligatory military service has lately been increased to four years.

To anyone with even a superficial knowledge of the Portuguese scene it will be obvious that this down-at-the-heel little country, kept afloat by NATO military aid (now mainly from West Germany) and by the grant of a privileged economic status within the European Free Trade community, is being steadily impoverished even further by its three colonial wars. And the main reason for this can only lie in the fighting success of the liberation movements in Guinea, Angola, and Mozambique.

But the main reason why Chaliand's book should be read is for its eyewitness account of two weeks spent inside "Portuguese" Guinea during the early summer of 1966. Together with the leader of its liberation movement, the forceful and ever-realistic

Amilcar Cabral, Chaliand crossed Senegal and Gambia (and then Senegal again) into the northern forests of Guinea on a tour of inspection, moved around in the area northwest of the Geba River, saw many guerrilla units and much of the movement's political, economic, and cultural work, and was able to record the views of a number of rank-and-file fighters, commanders, and civilians.

The resulting picture, rich in detail, is a most valuable account of a resistance movement in full and confident action. To the experienced eye, I think, this picture convincingly reveals a growth and expansion of resistance ("terrorism," in Portuguese terms) from the early heroism of small and isolated handfuls of hopeful men, hard-pressed and often terribly alone, to the installation of strong "interior bases" and the concomitant appearance of civilian organization in a liberated country.

To anyone who may still doubt whether Africans are "able" to organize guerrilla warfare and to exploit their successes right across the political spectrum, Chaliand's book will prove a surprise. What comes out of it is precisely the political competence of the movement's leadership and especially that of Cabral himself. There was, according to this sober factual account, no mere plunging ahead in the vague hope that the walls of Jericho would fall before a trumpet blast. Armed resistance was launched in 1963 only after years of political study and preparation.

Cabral and his fellow leaders carried out a most careful analysis of who was who, of the position of the Fulah and Mandingo chiefs vis-à-vis their village clientele, of the social structure of the town populations, of the opinions of those peoples who live in segmentary societies without chiefs, notably the Balantes, and of the ways in which Portuguese colonial exploitation actually affected the daily life of the country.

When Chaliand wrote this book in 1966–67, the African Independence Party of Guinea and the Cape Verde Islands (PAIGC) already controlled large rural areas from which they had chased the Portuguese police and army, and where they were installing their own new structures of independence. Now, two years later, the PAIGC has extended this control and reconstruction to at least two-thirds of the whole territory, and are driving the Portuguese out of their defensive camps and fortified garrisons. For an understanding of modern Africa, Chaliand's book is more timely than ever.

In Guinea a people entirely deprived of their natural rights have replied to the violence of imperial Portugal with a reluctant but saving violence of their own. They have recovered their own history, their right to make their own history. They have begun to shape this history for themselves after decades of painful subjection. They have rejoiced at what it means to see the future unfolding in their own arms and hearts. At a time when much of Africa is still deeply encoiled within the confusions and frustrations of structures both colonialist and neo-colonialist, these men and women of Guinea and the Cape Verde Islands have thought and fought their way through to new clarities, new freedoms, new objectives. Their country is only the size of Holland or Switzerland, but their story is as large as humanity. If it is little known, it ought to be widely known.

Chaliand has been well placed to tell this story. Long aware of its importance, he published his first account of the PAIGC and its aims and policies in 1964. During 1966 he traveled with Cabral and other PAIGC leaders through liberated territory in Guinea. There he collected firsthand impressions and biographies of PAIGC activists at all levels from the leadership to rank-and-file soldiers and political workers in the field. Judicious, careful of his facts, Chaliand offers much more than a reporter's notebook. He helps to situate this African war for independence within the wider struggle of our times: the struggle in which other peoples in other lands have reached out, and now reach out, for the means to turn our world toward survival, toward peace, toward hope.

Author's Foreword

With a total of more than 100,000 men deployed in Angola since 1961, in Guinea since 1963, and in Mozambique since 1964, Portugal, the last of the colonial powers, has been waging three simultaneous wars of repression in Africa. These wars are beginning to make a serious dent in the Portuguese economy, and in order to conduct them the Portuguese government must rely on the aid of its NATO allies, notably the United States and West Germany. In July 1966, 150,000 civil servants and military men received a pay increase of 20–25 percent in compensation for the rising cost of living. At the same time, the Secretary of the Portuguese Treasury stated that every year the military budget increased by five billion escudos[1] and that four and a half billion escudos were being spent to assure Portugal's economic growth. In 1967, "national defense and the protection of the nation's territorial integrity"—Portugal considers her colonies as overseas provinces —were the principal items on the Portuguese budget, of which nearly forty percent was allocated to war expenditures. Compulsory military service has been lengthened from eighteen months to four years. Until recently, emigration was offset by a favorable balance of payments, but now it has begun to create a shortage of skilled labor. And worse yet, the Portuguese authorities have been attempting to check a large-scale capital drainage caused by the state of general uneasiness among Portuguese investors who have started to place their holdings abroad.

The most important armed struggle on the African continent is presently taking place in "Portuguese" Guinea. Under the lead-

[1] One escudo equals about $.035. (Translators' note.)

ership of Amilcar Cabral, the forces of the PAIGC [2] have liberated more than half of their country. The experience of the PAIGC contradicts the Cuban *foco*[3] theory and demonstrates that, in this case, the armed struggle could not have been undertaken if a period of more than two years had not been devoted beforehand to preparatory political work. Which concrete methods permitted the initial mobilization of the peasant masses? What was the nature of the process through which they were won over to the cause? How are they organized? What is the function of political commissars, both within each combat unit and with respect to the population? How does a revolutionary leader like Cabral speak to the fighting men? Through what sort of discussion does he convince the peasants to intensify their participation in the struggle and to raise their level of production?

Guided by the practical experience of PAIGC guerrilla fighters and cadres and by their own evaluation of it, this book primarily offers answers to these questions.

The book's purpose is to outline the inner sociology of an African *maquis*. The leaders, cadres, guerrilla fighters, and peasants who at each of their various levels constitute the basic elements of a *maquis* have seldom before portrayed themselves either collectively or individually.

The book also proposes to consider the diverse experiences of the armed struggle in Africa and to draw a certain number of conclusions that can be applied elsewhere and that will constitute a valuable contribution to what we already know about the political strategy of guerrilla warfare in Southeast Asia and in Latin America.

---

[2] Partido Africano da Independencia da Guine e Cabo Verde: African Party for the Independence of Guinea and Cape Verde.

[3] A guerrilla unit which acts as the "focus" of an insurrection and which proceeds directly to the phase of armed struggle. See Che Guevara, *Guerrilla Warfare* (New York: Monthly Review Press, 1961).

PAIGC—PARTIDO AFRICANO DA INDEPENDENCIA
DA GUINE E CABO VERDE

Bulletin:

After inspecting the political organization and the armed forces in the southern and eastern regions of the country, Amilcar Cabral, secretary-general of our Party, has just spent two weeks in the northern regions of the country, where he presided over the semi-annual conference of cadres.

This conference took place in one of the liberated zones. It reached decisions about the following matters: intensification of the armed struggle during the rainy season, strengthening of the Party's political organization, increase of production, educational development, public health work, and the replenishment of supplies vital to the well-being of the masses.

During his stay in the north, the secretary-general of the Party inspected a number of schools, infirmaries, guerrilla bases, and units of our regular army. He attended rallies with audiences numbering in the hundreds and sometimes even the thousands, and was thus able to get a clear picture of the situation in our country and to discuss the prospects for our struggle and the future of our people.

The secretary-general was accompanied on his tour by Oswaldo Vieira (Ambrosio Djassi) and Francisco Mendes (Chico Te), who are members of the Political Committee and the Party leaders in the northern districts, as well as by José Mendes, a military representative of the Popular Movement for the Liberation of Angola (MPLA), and by Gérard Chaliand, a French journalist and writer (*Partisans* magazine).

When they learned of our secretary-general's presence in the area, the colonial forces made every effort to arrest or kill him. On June 5, at about 6 A.M., ten B-26 bombers and four Fiat fighters (the latter still bearing West German markings) bombed and strafed the village of Djagali where, the day before, the secretary-general had presided over a rally attended by more than 3,000 people. While this was going on, in an attempt to seal off all avenues of escape, the Portuguese sent gunboats and other vessels to patrol the Farim River, and six of their helicopters deposited troops on the Senegal border between Guidage and Bigène.

However, our troops prevented the Portuguese from accomplishing their intentions. Despite the bombing of Djagali, in which seven people died and five were injured, we drove the colonial forces out of the village, killing ten of their men and wounding several others. At the frontier, our forces routed the "air cavalry" troops, killing five colonialist soldiers and, once again, wounding several others.

June 9, 1966
The Conakry Headquarters of
the PAIGC Secretariat

Armed Struggle in Africa

1
Introduction

General Considerations

"Portuguese" Guinea occupies an area of 13,948 square miles between Senegal and the Republic of Guinea. In the northeastern region of Boe, its low tablelands form the last foothills of the Fouta-Djallon mountain range. In the center there is a forest zone, and in the south a coastal plain. In some places (Sucujaque, Cacheu, Bissau, Buba, Cacine), the sea penetrates deeply into the coastline and creates narrow, sharply sloping valleys. Inland beyond the salt-water limit, the major water basins are formed by the Farim, the Geba, and the Corubal rivers. Ships of 2,000 tons burden or less can navigate these rivers over distances of sixty to ninety-five miles. Guinea extends through a row of islands (the largest of which are Pecixe, Bissau, Bolama, and Como) and through the Bissagos Archipelago. Guinea's tropical climate has two seasons: the rainy season from June to November and the dry season during the remainder of the year. Its population has been estimated at 800,000, which comes to a density of fifty-seven inhabitants per square mile, a high figure for tropical Africa.[1]

The "Rios" of "Guiné e Cabo Verde" were among the first regions explored by Portugal in the mid-1400's. The Portuguese navigator Nuno Tristae sighted the mouths of the Farim and the Geba in 1446. In the ensuing years, the "Rios da Guiné" became the property of the benefactors and inhabitants of the Cape Verde Archipelago, located off the Senegal coast. Portuguese traders known as *lançados* set up posts along the shore. In 1630, the "captaincy-general of Cacheu" laid the groundwork of administrative occupation, and in 1692 a new "captaincy-general" of Bissau was

---

[1] For the most complete information available on Portuguese colonialism in Guinea, see Amilcar Cabral's *Report to the United Nations* (1962).

established to provide an administrative structure for the territory. The Portuguese went into the slave trade and were in the course of time to transport a certain number of their slaves to the Cape Verde Islands. The Pepels, a Bissau tribe, were usually in charge of sales.

In 1879, the Guinea and Cape Verde administration was dissolved. Threatened by British and French schemes after the Berlin treaty of 1884–85, the Portuguese endeavored to complete their conquest of the interior. With the help of the Islamized population, Teixeira Pinto subdued the Animist tribes and progressively cordoned off the entire country. Guinea was "pacified" after more than thirty years of military expeditions, but the final conquest of the Bissagos Archipelago did not take place until 1936. According to both the present constitution of Portugal, the law governing Portuguese overseas provinces, and the statute on political administration (ratified November 22, 1963, by Decree No. 45,-372), "Portuguese" Guinea constitutes one of Portugal's "overseas provinces" in Africa. Theoretically, Portuguese law provides for Guinea's administrative and financial autonomy. The governor is the highest-ranking official in the "province." He presides over the legislative council and is assisted by the government council. For the purposes of judicial administration, the "province" of Guinea constitutes a *comarca*, having its seat in Bissau and falling under the jurisdiction of Lisbon.

In point of fact, the law of the land for Guinea (until 1961, when it was rescinded) was the so-called native statute that provided the legal basis for a policy of apartheid by denying political rights to ninety-nine percent of the Guinean people. Article 2 of the statute stipulated that any member or descendant of the black race "who has not yet acquired the individual characteristics and social habits prerequisite to the full exercise of all the public and private rights of Portuguese citizenship, may not enjoy these rights." As a result, the "native" had no political rights: without the administration's approval, he could neither elect nor depose the traditional chiefs; he could not even change his place of residence without first applying for permission to do so. To make the transition from "native" to citizen, he had to have not only a speaking knowledge of Portuguese but also a job that permitted him to support himself and his dependents. Until the outbreak of the armed struggle, the Portuguese, in addition to levying a personal tax, also extracted forced labor.

Economic Survey

It would be superfluous to attempt to demonstrate the obvious economic exploitation constituted by Portugal's extraction of Guinea's wealth. On the eve of the war of national liberation, the Portuguese monopoly Companhia União Fabril (CUF) controlled all of Guinea's foreign trade. Portugal was the compulsory market for Guinean produce.

Table 1
Exports from "Portuguese" Guinea

Products	Amount (in tons)	To Portugal (percent)	To colonies (percent)	To other countries (percent)
Groundnuts (in shell)	74,000	99.96	0.04	0
Groundnuts (shelled)	28,000	100.00	0	0
Palm oil	1,260	100.00	0	0
Palm-cabbage	38,000	92.10	0	7.90
Wood	36,000	83.30	16.50	0.20
Rubber	270	100.00	0	0
Wax	348	95.10	0.30	0.60
Hides	1,059	100.00	0	0
Oil-cakes	1,480	15.60	0	84.40

Note: These figures apply to the peacetime period of 1958–60. For more detailed information, consult Cabral, cited above. This report provided the source material for part of my study *Guinée "portugaise" et Cap Vert en lutte pour leur indépendance* (Paris: François Maspero, 1964).

The country's most important products are rice, which is mainly reserved for home consumption, and groundnuts,[2] which provided the basis of Guinea's foreign trade. Thus, in the peacetime year of 1960, sixty percent of all foreign trade revenue came from groundnuts and seventy percent of the total production was exported. It should be noted that the cultivation of groundnuts was originally enforced by the Portuguese.

The following list indicates the distribution of cultivated areas:

Table 2
Major Crops

Crops	Acres	Percent	Production in tons
Hulled rice	308,170	25.86	90,247
Dry rice	69,815	5.86	10,030
Groundnuts	259,394	21.78	63,975
Millet	189,958	15.95	23,968
Sugar cane	130,678	10.97	17,834
Maize	61,278	5.15	7,994
Manioc	36,591	3.07	24,171

Source: Portuguese National Institute of Statistics, cited by Cabral.

After groundnuts, principal crop exports were palm oil, coconuts, rice, and wood (in the country's forests, Portugal has widely plundered the precious wood which provides an appreciable part of the revenue obtained from Guinean exports). Since rice is by far the most profitable crop, the PAIGC has been encouraging its cultivation since the outbreak of the armed struggle, and new areas have been cultivated in the liberated regions. Under Portuguese management, proceeds from groundnut sales seldom covered the cost of family labor. In the liberated regions, all agricultural produce is now consumed by the population. On the other hand, the war has noticeably depleted what used to be a large supply of livestock.

On the eve of the insurrection there were about 85,000 family

---

[2] Or peanuts. United Nations documents translate the French *arachide* as "groundnut," and so we have used that term throughout. (Translators' note.)

farmplots. The number of work units per family ranged between three and seven, whereas the total area under cultivation covered 13.5 percent of the territory or barely forty percent of the arable land. It should be pointed out that unlike Angola, for instance, Guinea has no plantation colonies. The essential part of Guinea's economy was in the hands of the Companhia União Fabril (CUF), which controlled foreign trade, and of the National Overseas Bank.[3] Industry is limited to about ten small factories, including three rice-husking factories, two groundnut processing factories, one paper-pulp factory, and two brick factories. There seems to be no mining at present, although there are deposits of bauxite and petroleum. It must be noted that, as opposed to Angola and Mozambique where the great international monopolies have widely entrenched themselves, Guinea is in general a truly Portuguese colony. Portuguese capitalism largely rests on the exploitation of colonial peoples. Although Portugal itself, once a semi-colony of England, managed during World War II to lay the foundations of an industrial system dominated by national monopolies, today it is becoming more and more dependent on the great international monopolies. In the competition among the latter, West Germany leads Great Britain, the United States, and France.

It is also interesting to note that Portugal's heavily adverse balance of trade shows a surplus only for the African colonies. (See Table 3.)

	Annual deficit (in millions of escudos)	*Deficit increase* (in millions of escudos)
1962	6,198	—
1963	6,842	664 (10.4%)
1964	7,067	225 (3.3%)

In 1965, Portuguese imports from West Germany totalled 4,200 million escudos, whereas exports only amounted to 1,308 million

[3] See Appendix for a list of foreign interests (Portuguese and non-Portuguese) in Guinea.

Table 3

Trade with Principal Countries and Territories

(in millions of escudos)

Countries and Territories	1960			1964		
	Import	Export	Balance	Import	Export	Balance
Overseas Colonies						
Angola	851	1,237	+ 386	1,857	2,167	+ 310
Mozambique	1,157	845	− 312	1,057	1,205	+ 148
Others	245	324	+ 79	315	384	+ 69
Total	2,253	2,406	+ 153	3,229	3,756	+ 527
Western Europe						
Austria	91	46	− 45	199	148	− 51
Belgium/Luxemburg	935	289	− 646	713	384	− 329
Denmark	71	136	+ 65	152	313	+ 161
France	1,307	319	− 988	1,559	730	− 829
Greece	15	42	+ 27	109	82	− 27
Holland	509	246	− 263	655	404	− 251
Iceland	71	1	− 70	96	7	− 89
Italy	570	325	− 245	974	424	− 550
Norway	126	84	− 42	132	132	−
Spain	138	95	− 43	448	451	+ 3
Sweden	365	268	− 97	441	524	+ 83
Switzerland	615	119	− 496	788	272	− 516
Turkey	2	8	+ 6	383	44	− 339
United Kingdom	1,868	1,284	− 584	2,967	2,331	− 636
West Germany	2,677	857	−1,820	3,334	1,106	−2,228

	1960			1964		
Eastern Europe	225	206	— 19	277	196	— 81
Americas						
Brazil	74	67	— 7	153	41	— 112
Canada	99	96	— 3	116	235	+ 119
Curaçao	225	5	— 220	119	1	— 118
Mexico	45	46	+ 1	52	39	— 13
United States	1,152	1,049	— 103	2,290	1,549	— 741
Venezuela	146	52	— 94	45	58	+ 13
Africa						
Algeria	7	49	+ 42	48	8	— 40
Morocco	132	212	+ 80	135	146	+ 11
Republic of South Africa	112	79	— 33	139	158	+ 19
Asia and Oceania						
Australia	78	76	— 2	97	98	+ 1
Federation of Malaysia	112	3	— 109	66	9	— 57
Iran	59	17	— 42	73	11	— 62
Iraq	744	20	— 724	584	33	— 551
Israel	30	118	+ 88	22	97	+ 75
Japan	249	61	— 188	43	131	+ 88
New Zealand	56	16	— 40	132	20	+ 112
Pakistan	44	17	— 27	127	37	— 90
Other countries, foreign ships, etc.	493	694	+ 201	1,184	839	— 345
Total	13,442	7,002	— 6,440	18,652	11,058	— 7,594
TOTAL	15,695	9,408	— 6,287	21,881	14,814	— 7,067

Source: For 1960, *OECD Bulletin;* for 1964, *Monthly Bulletin of the National Institute of Statistics.*

escudos. Three countries account for fifty percent of Portugal's entire foreign trade deficit:

	Value (in millions of escudos)	Percent of deficit
Germany	2,228	29.4
France	829	10.9
United States	741	9.8
	3,798	50.1

In order to conduct the war, Portugal receives substantial aid from its NATO allies, notably West Germany and the United States. Moreover, these two countries have very large interests in the mining resources of Angola and Mozambique.

Portugal's balance of payments with its colonies continued to be favorable in 1965. (See Table 4.)

With half of the country controlled by the PAIGC, comprehensive statistics for the Guinean economy have been unavailable during the past few years. However, the monthly bulletin of Portugal's National Institute for Statistics gives some interesting information. In 1959, Guinea and Cape Verde supplied 16.3 percent of Portugal's colonial imports; in 1963, 11.5 percent; and in 1964, 9.8 percent. Portuguese exports to Guinea and Cape Verde went down from 12.1 percent in 1959 to 10.7 percent in 1963 and 10.2 percent in 1964.

According to the PAIGC, the Companhia União Fabril has had to close most of its stores in the regions that have not yet been liberated, and several of its boats have been seized, along with their cargoes. The Overseas Trading Company has given up all of its Guinean business, in the bushlands as well as the towns. Billiton Maatschappij N.V., the Dutch company which holds a concession for mining the Boe bauxite deposits, has been forced to suspend its exploratory operations because of PAIGC activity.

In Guinea, Portugal has not found war to be a paying proposition. In 1966, Portugal's foreign trade deficits were increasing, not only overall, but even with respect to the African colonies.

Table 4

Metropolitan Portugal's Balance of Payments with Its Overseas Provinces in 1965

(in millions of escudos)

Transactions	Angola		Mozambique		Others		Total		Balance
	Debit	Credit	Debit	Credit	Debit	Credit	Debit	Credit	
A. Current Transactions	3,933	4,587	1,379	3,714	1,046	1,281	6,358	9,582	+3,224
1. Merchandise	1,467	2,349	1,019	1,830	186	658	2,672	4,837	+2,165
2. Invisible (Services)	2,466	2,238	360	1,884	860	623	3,686	4,745	+1,059
a. Travel	6	239	6	187	—	35	12	461	+ 449
b. Income from investments	31	458	9	351	822	57	40	866	+ 826
c. Public sector	2,352	568	292	571	22	255	3,466	1,394	−2,072
d. Shipping and other services	47	388	15	259	16	56	84	703	+ 619
e. Private transfers	30	585	38	516	145	220	84	1,321	+1,237
B. Capital Transactions	188	—	—	83			—	—	− 250
1. Short-term capital (net)		53		27	18				+ 62
2. Long-term capital	457	216	588	644	201	74	1,246	934	− 312
a. Private sector	170	113	77	162	19	30	266	305	+ 39
b. Public sector	287	103	511	482	182	44	980	629	− 351
C. Transactions Not Accounted for and Errors	—	6	14	—	21	—	—	—	− 29
D. Total	472	472	2,404	2,404	69	69	—	—	+2,945
E. Financing									−2,945
1. Multilateral transactions	34		16			50			
2. Net change in short term assets [increase (−)]		524	136		275				+ 113
3. Clearing account in Portugal [credit (−), debit (+)]	962		2,252			161			−3,053
4. Reserve account in the overseas provinces [credit (+), debit (−)]					5				− 5

Source: OECD *Bulletin*, 1965.

Society and Social Structure

"Portuguese" Guinea numbers about 800,000 inhabitants. Its population is made up of various ethnic groups.

Balantes	250,000
Mandjaks	140,000
Fulahs	100,000
Mandingos	80,000
Pepels	50,000
Mancags or Brames	35,000
Felupes	15,000
Bissagos	15,000

There are also other less numerous ethnic groups such as the Beofadas, the Baïrotes, the Cassangas, the Banhuns, the Sarakollé, the Balantes-Manés, and the Pajadincas.

Behind these tribal and linguistic divisions, however, there is one fundamental ethnic cleavage: that which separates the Islamized groups from the Animists.

The Animists belong to a large ethnic bloc which extends along the coast from Senegal to the Ivory Coast. Its characteristic feature is the absence of a higher form of state organization. With the notable exception of the Mandjaks, the Animists (who account for approximately seventy percent of the population) live in societies without a system of customary chieftainships; age groups seem to constitute the major social distinction. The village community system shows far fewer signs of degeneration among the Animists than among the Muslims. This contrast between the groups obviously existed long before Portuguese colonization, and the two groups differ economically, socially, and religiously. On the other hand, on the eve of the colonial conquest, private ownership of the land did not exist anywhere in Guinea, nor had the monetary system been introduced.

The Balantes are the most numerous ethnic group of "Portuguese" Guinea (thirty percent of the total population), and are the most representative of the Animists. The pivot on which Balante social life turns is the family cell, or *morança*, which is the branch of a single family. In this context, patriarchal authority is preponderant. In effect, the social organization common to all the Animist tribes of Guinea is based on age groups, as follows:

Nfar, or Infar	10 to 12 years
Mpebe	13 to 15 ”
Ncumane	16 to 20 ”
N'hai, or Blufo	21 to 25 ”

After this age, circumcision is practiced as it is (albeit much earlier) among the Muslims; the Animists do not, however, practice excision. After circumcision, one is *lante* (adult) and is initiated into the secrets of the group, thereby acquiring the right to appropriate land within the context of the village community. The older a man grows, the more he is respected, and the *homem grande*, or old man, enjoys special prestige. Moreover, one is the more powerful in proportion to the number of hands in one's family. Polygamy exists but is not at all widespread among the Animists. Besides, the Animist woman enjoys relative freedom. If she is widowed, she does not automatically become, as elsewhere, the wife of the deceased's brother. She can decide her own future and may remarry at the end of a year.

In addition to the patriarchal authority governing the family cell, there exists at the village level a constituted social authority: the council of elders. This gerontocracy regulates the distribution of land and settles whatever disputes may arise according to the laws of the group. There is no authority from outside the village. Loose ties do exist between Balante villages, based on the community of language, beliefs, and customs.

The division of arable land is primarily tribal: there is a Balante "zone," just as there are Fulah and Mandjak zones. But the property rights to the land are held by each individual village. The products of agriculture, however, as well as the instruments of production, belong to the head of the family—a fact that clearly differentiates this mode of production from that of the primitive community, which has everywhere disappeared and yet is wishfully seen by some as the basis for an African rural "socialism."

As mentioned earlier, the Balantes are noteworthy as growers of rice, usually by the wet paddy method. A large proportion of the group lives along the coast (much of which consists of rice paddies), and their lands have often been conquered from the swamps.

From the religious point of view, one notices the absence of a clergy among the Balantes. Like most of the other Animist tribes, they worship a creator-god and various intermediate deities associated with rain, agriculture, and the like.

The Portuguese imposed on the Balantes alien chiefs recruited from the Islamized tribes, but the Balantes never accepted them. This explains, in part at least, the fact that the mobilization and participation of the Balantes in the armed struggle have been massive.

The Mandjaks are generally considered to be a transitional group between the two main groups. As Animists, they have retained the characteristic Animist age classes, but they seem to have an increasing tendency to define social distinctions in terms of economic structures that bear a resemblance to those of the Islamized group. From a social point of view, the Mandjaks are visibly creating the embryo of a customary chieftainship system.[4] In contrast to the other Animist ethnic groups, they have a clergy invested with religious and political functions.

The Islamized groups, which account for approximately thirty percent of the population, are the Fulahs and the Mandingos, and their societies function under the system of customary chieftainships. Their mode of production has sometimes wrongly been called "feudal"; in any event, it has reached a more advanced stage of historical evolution than that of the Animists. Social distinctions are well defined, and a system of patriarchal slavery also exists. The Fulahs and Mandingos have counterparts in the Republic of Guinea as well as in Senegal.

The Fulahs belong to the huge Peul family, which extends over all of western Africa. Those in "Portuguese" Guinea seem less culturally and economically advanced than their neighbors, the Fouta-Djallon Fulahs of the Republic of Guinea, who had a powerful empire in the seventeenth century. The Fulahs were

---

[4] This analysis summarizes the principal points developed in my pamphlet *Guinée "portuguaise" et Cap Vert* (cited above), pp. 17–26.

originally nomadic shepherds, and although they are now sedentary shepherds and farmers, the pastoral foundations of their poetry and their cosmogony are still very much in evidence. The existence of a form of state structure indicates that the Fulahs have passed through a process of marked social differentiation. Their social organization is based on customary chiefs, who descend from great aristocratic families, such as the Diallos and the Sows. Besides the chiefs and their families, there are the lords. The chiefs, who can come only from the aristocratic stratum, exact tribute in kind and exercise economic, religious, and military prerogatives.

Beneath the aristocratic class of Fulah society stand political and religious chiefs, farmers, and then a series of trade-castes, such as those of the goldsmiths and weavers. Blacksmiths and *griots*[5] make up the lower castes. As noted above, there is widespread domestic slavery. The formerly effective village community system has very badly disintegrated and the customary chiefs have proceeded to an unequal parcelling off of land to poor peasants, while leaving the nobles in full private possession of family lands. The Portuguese have given the Fulahs, who are spread out all over the country, a large measure of privilege, in order to make their ruling class an instrument of indirect domination over the Animist tribes. From the standpoint of social structures—though with a less pronounced differentiation—the Mandingos are quite close to the Fulahs. It is from these two ethnic groups that the greatest number of itinerant merchants are recruited.

The Islamized tribes live in round huts huddled together in the center of a cultivated area. The Animists, on the other hand, live in rectangular huts dispersed around the outskirts of their fields. Livestock was plentiful before the war and was concentrated for the most part in the hands of the Fulahs, the Mandingos, and the Balantes. The phenomenon of hoarding through the accumulation of livestock and the refusal to put it to commercial use is seen here as elsewhere in West Africa.

---

[5] A type of African poet and itinerant musician. The *griots* constitute a special caste. They are often thought to have supernatural powers: hence they are both feared and respected. Since they live outside the traditional social organization, they are often chosen to arbitrate disputes between individuals or tribes. (Translators' note.)

The Islamized groups use the "Marabout" alphabet. The Animists have no written language. (Ninety-nine percent of Guinea's people are illiterate—it should be mentioned that in the entire colonial period, fourteen Guineans have received the equivalent of a B.A. degree.) Creole (Africanized Portuguese) is the language commonly spoken by a part of the population, especially in the urban areas.

In "Portuguese" Guinea, forced labor was used on a relatively small scale, chiefly in road construction and maintenance—in contrast to Angola where the Portuguese imposed the obligation of working on the European plantations. Inland in Guinea there were only a few Portuguese administrators and merchants. Only a small proportion of the land was private property, and a part of that (some 4,000 square kilometers) belonged to the Portuguese Banco Nacional Ultramarino and CUF. A few Africans are proprietors of *pontas*, small farms where they cultivate sugar cane in order to distill spirits.

From an economic point of view, the people who played an essential part in production at the outbreak of the liberation war were the Balantes, the Fulahs, the Mandingos, and the Mandjaks. The Balantes seem to be the major rice-growers in the present liberated regions (although every group throughout the country cultivates rice) and along with the Fulahs and the Mandingos are the primary producers of groundnuts.

Social classes in the countryside

Social classes in the countryside closely parallel the social classes within the different tribes. They divide as follows:

—The important Fulah or Mandingo chiefs who were imposed by the Portuguese or agreed to be their agents. Since the extension of the liberated regions, these chiefs have placed themselves under the protection of the colonial authorities.

—Great noble families of Fulah, Mandingo, and marginally Mandjak origin. Often, notably among the Fulahs, these families have gone over to the Portuguese side.

—A marginal category of small farmers. These proprietors of *pontas* have for the most part come over to the PAIGC.

—The itinerant merchants, or Djoulas. This category cannot thrive outside the context of a monetary economy, the suppression of which in the liberated regions has caused their attitude toward the struggle to remain ambiguous. Certain elements work simultaneously for the Portuguese and for the PAIGC. Experience proves that in the context of independence, the Djoulas, by virtue of their enterprising spirit and thrift, rapidly develop into a lower middle class of shopkeepers and merchants which tends to ally itself with the bureaucratic bourgeoisie.

—The rural artisans, who in the liberated regions have maintained close ties with their villages and consequently collaborate with the PAIGC.

—The peasants, among whom differences exist to a more important degree than one might at first notice. Among the Animists (with the exception of the Mandjaks) there is no accumulation of property. In contrast with the Muslims, a pre-capitalist mentality continues to prevail even today. Wealth is disposed of in great feasts or potlatches. There is no ambition to rise above the group, for this would amount to becoming separated from it. This stems from, among other things, the almost total lack of any internal monetary exchange. In the context of the present struggle, the Animists are obviously the ones who suffered least from the disappearance of any monetary economy in the liberated regions. The Animist peasants, moreover, participate much more fully in the struggle. Indeed, as we have already pointed out, the Balantes threw themselves into the struggle from the outset. In the first place, the Portuguese had imposed on the chiefless society of the Balantes, Muslim chiefs who in the name of the colonial administration subjected them to a double exploitation. In the second place, unlike the Fulahs and the Mandingos, who were partially dependent for their livelihood on commerce—and more precisely on smuggling—with Senegal, the solely agricultural Balantes underwent total exploitation when the Portuguese came to levy a tax in kind. Finally, among the Balantes bravery is traditionally a much celebrated virtue.[6] The Mandjaks, although held back at the outset by those of their chiefs who were in league with the

---

[6] Theft is considered, particularly among the adolescents, an achievement, all the more glorious if it is committed under dangerous circumstances.

Portuguese, quickly joined the struggle. On the other hand, a very sharply defined resistance to liberation manifested itself among the Fulahs, where the influence of traditional chiefs entirely devoted to Portuguese colonialism remains strong. Certain Fulah elements have responded to the alignment of forces created by the PAIGC through the armed struggle by joining the liberation movement, whereas others have withdrawn to regions still controlled by the Portuguese. Nonetheless, because of the social structure, a conflict of interest persists between the Fulah ruling class and the rest of the population, especially the Animists. This contradiction will not totally disappear until the Fulah aristocratic classes have been liquidated by the Fulahs themselves. Finally, the Mandingos of the liberated regions, although they have rallied to the anti-colonial struggle, are particularly sensitive—in the north, at least—to the disappearance of the money economy.

In general, at the outset of the struggle the peasants displayed reticence and reserve, a reaction resulting from conditions peculiar to peasantry of tropical Africa. This peasantry—outside the countries or zones with plantations using hired day labor—is for the most part not faced with the problem of agrarian reform. The land is abundant and, for better or worse, permits a subsistence economy. But colonialism provided many other objective conditions around which to mobilize the people. It was the task of the PAIGC to demonstrate that it was possible to fight the Portuguese successfully in order to draw the people into the struggle.

Social classes in the towns

There are five towns of any importance in Guinea. It is there that the Portuguese civilians live, 3,000 of them in 1960; there were no "poor whites" among them. Bissau, the capital, has 25,000 inhabitants; Bafata, 10,000; Bissora, 5,000; Mansoa, 5,000; and Bolama, 5,000. These figures date from before the war and have probably changed with population shifts. Toward these cities gravitate large numbers of the population, for whom they are a center of attraction.

In the African urban scene, one can distinguish the following classes and socio-economic levels:

—A handful of high officials, especially from Cape Verde, who are among those classed as *assimilados*. But their number is so small (perhaps a dozen) that it is not even possible to consider them a class. It is worth noting, however, that one of the great differences between Portuguese colonialism and the colonialism of other European powers is the existence of such *assimilados*, a social category the Portuguese regard as integrated into Portuguese society. The *assimilado* becomes a citizen; he is no longer a "native." This category was used by the Portuguese as an instrument of indirect domination.

—The lower middle class: middle- and lower-ranking government employees; bank, business, and store clerks; small merchants. This class, including family members, numbers roughly 10,000 (1.5 percent of the total population).

If the rural lower middle class rallied almost as a matter of course to the liberation movement, in the measure to which the economy was biased against it, the attitude of their urban counterparts has been much more ambiguous. This urban group depended entirely on the colonial presence and feared that it would lose the economic and social advantages it had thus far acquired, even though it was interested in the prospect of an independence in which it could substitute itself for the white colonists.

Three main currents may be discerned in the political make-up of this lower midle class: (1) A minority group, generally consisting of government employees or merchants having close ties with the Portuguese, which has been enriched by the war thanks to the concrete help they have furnished to the PIDE (political police). (2) The majority of the lower middle class, long hesitant but now—with the passage of time and the victories of the liberation movement—timidly engaged in the struggle while preparing to be the major beneficiaries of independence because they think of themselves as irreplaceable experts and organizers. Meanwhile, the struggle is in the process of forming numerous experts and organizers in the interior, as well as abroad. (3) A group that, like the first, is a minority (although somewhat larger), but from which has emerged the hardcore leadership of the struggle. It is this group, consisting for the most part of minor government and business employees, that began the struggle and continues to direct it.

—Wage-laborers, those who sell their labor power on a day-to-day basis and do not constitute a working class in the classical sense of the term—numbering about 25,000 to 30,000. They are workers in repair shops, chauffeurs and truck drivers, domestic servants, street vendors, dockworkers, and various day-laborers in trucking and river transport. (These latter, the dock and other transport workers, comprise the most conscious element; it was they who were behind the strikes of 1956 and 1959.) Wage-laborers on the whole were prompt to join the struggle. It should be noted that they often retain a peasant mentality; it is moreover a well-known phenomenon that in tropical Africa the city-country migration still moves in both directions. It has also been noticed that the mechanics, accustomed to precise and painstaking work, have an excellent sense of organization and discipline. Very often, they have made remarkable cadres of middle rank at the heart of the guerrilla struggle.

—The lumpenproletariat, arising from the rural exodus. It is hard to specify the size of this class, especially since the beginning of the war. The men loaf around, puttering at this and that, working occasionally by the day when they can. Their women are often prostitutes. There is a tendency here as elsewhere in tropical Africa to swarm around a member of the family who is making a regular salary. The experience of the PAIGC struggle has shown that this category is often reactionary. The PIDE has many informers and other agents in this class and does not seem to have much trouble in recruiting reinforcements.

The city youth poses a very special problem—and this seems to be the case in numerous cities in western Africa. This urban fringe group, which represents a very substantial proportion of the youth in the towns of Guinea, is characterized by the fact that it belongs neither to the wage-laborers nor to the lumpenproletariat. Its members have a certain amount of education; they have mastered Portuguese; they work occasionally or are supported by the relatives with whom they live; they have no definite profession. They are a temporary proletariat with a lower-middle-class mentality. Nonconformist, restless, unstable, they aspire to a better life and are sensitive to the constraints of colonialism. These young people have turned out to be particularly mobilizable in the struggle. They have played and continue to play an important role in the urban struggle, as well as in the agitation reaching out into the countryside. A substantial part of the middle rank cadres in the PAIGC has come from this social group.

The Struggle of the PAIGC

In September 1956, Amilcar Cabral and his circle secretly founded the PAIGC in Bissau. Before this, the African petty bourgeoisie, which provided the backbone of the Party's leadership, had sought above all to climb socially by means of assimilation. Only a few of the 8,000 *assimilados* living in Guinea at the time were interested in a re-Africanization of their country and in the idea of national independence. For the most part, these were persons who were or had been university students in Portugal and had been active, together with their Angolan and Mozambican counterparts, in founding the Center for African Studies. After 1954, this petty bourgeoisie began to lose whatever illusions it had had about the possibility of a modus vivendi within the colonial context. At that moment, the Portuguese were about to ban the athletic and cultural associations the Africans were trying to set up.

The Portuguese political police (PIDE) made their first appearance in Guinea in 1957. The Party apparatus was built up with corresponding secrecy and care. Security was guaranteed by a strict compartmentalization in cells of three to five members each. Originally organized and manned by the radical fringe of the petty bourgeoisie, the Party's ranks were soon swelled by river-transport workers and Bissau dockworkers. The movement spread from the capital inland to the towns of Bolama and Bafata. Little by little, the idea of independence and of a struggle shared by Guinea and Cape Verde became popularized among the urban masses.

On August 3, 1959, colonial troops put down a dock strike in Pidjiguiti and killed fifty workers. A month later, the Party held a meeting in Bissau at which it decided to lay the groundwork for the armed struggle and to concentrate on mobilizing the peasantry in the countryside, future scene of the guerrilla war. Guinea was divided into six regions and these were divided into zones. By the beginning of 1960, militants were out in the countryside trying to get the work of explanation and mobilization under way. At the same time, a whole series of small nationalist groups sprang up spontaneously in Bissau. One of them was headed by Rafael Barbosa, who later became chairman of the PAIGC. In his initial capacity as secretary of the Party control commission, he organized the Oïo and Bafata regions and trained the nucleus that was to spark the outbreak of the armed struggle.

The first wave of repression struck the Party in 1960 and the struggle entered its most difficult phase. Amilcar Cabral, the Party's secretary-general, moved to Conakry, where he established a school for training cadres who subsequently returned home to work in the countryside. They in turn sent back new recruits to take their places at the school.

In April 1961, the Conference of Nationalist Organizations of Portuguese Colonies (CONCP) was formed in Casablanca, its seat to be in Rabat. Although the armed struggle had already begun in Angola, the PAIGC was still meticulously laying the groundwork for the political conditions which would permit it to be launched in Guinea. On the night of June 30–July 1, 1962, a series of sabotage raids was carried out from bases inside Guinea. Police repression had intensified: as early as March, Rafael Barbosa and a hundred other militants had been arrested in Bissau. Toward the end of July 1962, before the anniversary of the Pidjiguiti massacre, the Portuguese arrested 2,000 persons in Bissau and declared the city under martial law. In August and September 1962, the fourth conference of Party cadres convened in Conakry and decided to expand the armed struggle at all costs. So it came about that by January 1963 a broad guerrilla campaign had been launched in the southern half of the country. The fact was soon acknowledged by the Portuguese high command. General Gomes de Araujo, the Portuguese Minister of Defense, declared: "Sizable and well-armed groups, trained in subversive warfare in North Africa and the Communist countries, have made incursions on Guinean territory in a zone comprising fifteen percent of its area." [7] But a second "zone of insecurity" was already being created in the north of the country, and by the end of the year the PAIGC estimated that it controlled nearly one-third of the national territory.

In February 1964, a Party Congress was held in the *maquis* and a reorganization was effected. By the beginning of 1963, the struggle was being waged on three levels:

—*Economic:* Systematic destruction of CUF warehouses. Lowering of groundnut export production. Increase of rice production for local consumption.

—*Political:* Installation of military bases in the forest but not in the villages—so as to avoid the repressions that would otherwise be automatically levelled against the peasantry. At the same time, continued political work in the villages.

—*Military:* Ceaseless harassment of the enemy in order to create a permanent atmosphere of demoralizing insecurity.

In view of the new conditions created by the struggle, the 1964 Congress decided to:

1) Divide the country up into regions and zones around strategic bases.

2) Modify the Party's political structure (see below).

3) Rationally organize the liberated regions so as to replace the Portuguese administratively and economically; in the south, create a system of people's stores.

4) Reorganize militarily: to strengthen cohesion, no more autonomous regions or zones. Henceforth, everything must be closely tied to the Party's central leadership. In effect, autonomy had given rise to petty local potentates who, in the name of the Party, had shown a tendency to usurp broad powers over the population.

5) Create a regular army, the FARP (People's Revolutionary Armed Forces), in addition to the local village guerrilla militias.

On the whole, the political structure of the Party remains as determined by the 1964 Congress, and consists of: (1) The Political Bureau. 20 members—15 regulars and 5 alternates—including an

---

[7] *Diario de Lisboa*, July 18, 1963.

executive committee of 7 members. (2) The Central Committee. 65 members—including 20 alternates—divided into 7 departments: armed forces political action; foreign affairs; political control of military cadres and of the Party apparatus; secretariat for the training of cadres, information and propaganda; security; economy and finances; development and coordination of mass organizations.

In April 1964, the Portuguese attempted to launch a broad counteroffensive. They attacked the liberated island of Como, which strategically commands the entire south of the country. After sixty-five days, 3,000 Portuguese troops, backed up by air support, were unable to retake the island and had to withdraw after losing several hundred men. The materiel at the disposal of the PAIGC, supplied by various sources, had been considerably reinforced since 1963 and heavy artillery had become more and more abundant.

In 1965, the liberated zones already covered half the country. Bases had been strengthened in both manpower and materiel, while the Portuguese troops had been inactive for several months. Air strikes became the principal Portuguese tactic against the liberated regions,[8] where in certain zones no taxes had been paid for two years. The creation of a political structure in villages where Party committees had been elected was under way. Although the armed struggle in that year declined slightly, its results, as published in a PAIGC communiqué of August 4, 1965, were 1,500 Portuguese dead or wounded, dozens of military vehicles destroyed, three airplanes shot down.

Meanwhile, Portuguese troops, which had numbered 10,000 in 1962, were increased to 25,000. In Angola, a territory thirty times larger, there are less than three times that number. Five chiefs of staff succeeded one another in Guinea without being able to bring the situation under control.

The year 1966 was characterized by an intensification of the struggle during the rainy season and, more particularly, by attacks on and systematic destruction of Portuguese garrisons and fortified

---

[8] This repression by air attack caused the emigration of 56,000 Guineans across the northern frontier into Senegal. In 1967, the UN High Commission for Refugees contributed some thirty-five million francs CFA (about $140,000) to the assistance program for Guinean refugees.

camps. PAIGC military bases were reduced in size to promote greater mobility. Schools were integrated with the villages. At this writing, a third front has been opened in the east of the country. Until the end of 1966, the country was divided into two inter-regions, north and south, with the following regional structure:

Northern interregion, divided into seven regions, in turn divided into zones:

São Domingos: Susana and N'Gore.

Farim: Sambuya and Candjanabari.

Canchungo: Bassarel, Churo, and Cayo.

Oïo: Biambi, Morès, and Sara.

Bafata: Geba and Canhãmina.

Bissau: Quinhamel, Safim, and Bissau.[9]

Gabu: limits not yet settled.

The north, comprising sixty percent of the country, is bordered on the interior by the Geba River as far as Bafata, by the Bafata-Gabu road, and by the Gabu-Kabuka road as far as the Corubal River. It is about 7,780 square miles in area; each of the regions composing it covers roughly 1,170 square miles.

Southern interregion, divided into six regions: Catio, Fula-cunda-Bolama, the Bissagos Archipelago, and an autonomous region (for military purposes only) in the extreme southeast: Quita-fine, Xitolie, and Boe.

Each region has the following zones:

Catio: Cubucare, Komo, Cufar, Cubisseco, Fronteira.

Fulacunda-Bolama: Bolama, Quinara, N'Djassani.

Bissagos Archipelago: Not yet divided into zones.

Quitafine: All one zone, but having regional status.

Boe

Xitolie[10]

It was in the last two regions, Boe and Xitolie, that the third, eastern front was opened.

The basic structure everywhere is the village committee, formed and elected by the villagers themselves. Then comes the zone com-

---

[9] The island of Bissau, 1,500 square kilometers in area, remains entirely under Portuguese control.

[10] Chaliand does not indicate whether these latter regions were ever to be divided into zones. (Translators' note.)

mittee, in which village representatives participate; then the regional committee; and, finally, the interregional committee under direct Party control.

The PAIGC has encountered—and has generally overcome—numerous difficulties in the course of the struggle, difficulties that were, from the very outset, connected with contradictions springing from the existing patriarchal and tribal structures and, more specifically, with a persistent tendency toward the passive acceptance of the authority vested in local leaders or chiefs. These difficulties first appeared during the phase of mobilization, when the tribal chiefs maintained their ties with the Portuguese, and during the period when autonomy permitted certain local leaders of the armed struggle to develop authoritarian tendencies. Thus while the Party has progressively extended its political control into every area of activity, it has at the same time tried to reinforce the autonomy of the regularly elected village committees.

The Party has persistently undertaken political action to smooth out tribal contradictions, especially those existing between the Fulah elements and the rest of the population—chiefly the Animists. In the course of the struggle, by dint of endless explanation, magico-religious beliefs and practices have lost much of their importance. The major contradiction is still the relatively low level of productive forces, with its attendant ignorance and excessively slow rhythm of work, itself a product of the rapport between African man and nature. In this regard, as in the modification of social structures, the armed struggle has been a stimulant and an accelerator of prime importance, to the extent that the Party has always accompanied military activity with political work.

For the Portuguese, the war is already lost. In order to win the struggle imposed upon them by the militants of the PAIGC, the colonial troops would have had to put into practice the major principles of counter-insurgency:[11] beat the guerrillas militarily; detach the population from the guerrillas; restore governmental authority throughout the country and recreate viable economic and social

---

[11] T. N. Greene, ed., *The Guerrilla and How to Fight Him. Selections from the Marine Corps Gazette* (New York: Praeger, 1962); Peter Paret and J. W. Shy, *Guerrilla in the Nineteen-Sixties* (New York: Praeger, 1962).

conditions. The Portuguese are not capable of doing any of this. In political terms, they have already been beaten. However, they do hold towns, large settlements, and isolated garrisons within the liberated regions.

In the immediate and near future, the PAIGC can increase and extend its control over regions it does not yet control, render impossible all highway and river travel throughout the country, and destroy the remaining Portuguese posts. The Portuguese would then be left with the cities, the important towns, and a few very well-fortified camps. At this stage, if local or international conditions do not bring the Portuguese to negotiate politically, it is clear that the People's Revolutionary Armed Forces (FARP) would be obliged to make a considerable qualitative leap forward to transform the present Portuguese tactical retreat into total military defeat.

2

With the Maquis

On the Other Side of the Farim

At one o'clock in the morning we left the Casamance behind and stepped over the border into "Portuguese" Guinea.

We had left Dakar by car at the beginning of the previous afternoon. There were eight of us: the drivers, who were also PAIGC militants; two nurses returning from a training course; José Mendes, a military representative from the MPLA (Popular Movement for the Liberation of Angola), who was on his way to study the techniques employed in the armed struggle by the Guinean *maquis*; and Amilcar Cabral, secretary-general of the Party. We made our way across the tiny enclave of Gambia, a former British colony on the banks of the river that bears its name. Cotton goods, English cigarettes, and Scotch whisky are sold there. The men earn a living mainly as traders or traffickers. Like the Casamance River, the Gambia must be crossed by ferry in Senegalese territory. Shortly after midnight, we came to a lonely field at the edge of a forest. As soon as we arrived, a dozen soldiers armed with machine guns came out of their hiding place. They were FARP fighters led by Oswaldo, the man in charge of military affairs in the northern interregion. Then some peasants came to take away our baggage.

There was enough light so that we could easily see several yards ahead. The vast sky was studded with stars, and the mugginess already in the air indicated that the rainy season could not be far off. We kept up a good, firm pace over the path leading across the wooded savannah. From time to time the moon would disappear, but thanks to someone's flashlight we could tell the direction to go in. We marched on silently, in single file, and at the same steady pace. Every half-mile or so, FARP lookout men came out of their

29

hiding places, guns slung over their shoulders, and greeted us as we passed. By now we could feel the midnight dampness clinging to our shirts.

We marched on through a much more thickly wooded area and from time to time Cabral would point out villages that had been destroyed by bombings and deserted by Balantes who had taken shelter in the Oïo forest. We went by four of these villages. The night became even darker and we continued to meet FARP lookouts. During the night we were to see more than fifty of them. At 3:30, we stopped not far from a spring, where we rested briefly and had a drink of water. We set off again. The path became narrower; young plam trees, their leaves fanning out around us, twanged like bowshots as we brushed them aside. Once there had been a lot of game around there, but the bombings drove it away toward the Casamance.

Around 5:30, we came to the Cacheu River, which is also known as the Farim. It is a wide river with thick vegetation on its banks. We had to cross it by canoe at daybreak. In some places the river pierces through its banks and burrows canals fifty yards deep. These canals are lined with mangroves which dip their branches so far into the water that they actually take root there. Sometimes as many as twenty or thirty branches of one mangrove lie twisted in the water, and the tree seems to shoot forth from this tower of roots. The canoe made smooth headway through the underwater forest. Bird cries punctuated the dawn silence.

On the other side of the river, the sun was already up. Another FARP unit was waiting to receive us. Before long we skirted a village. A woman from the village committee came up to Oswaldo, greeted him, and invited him and his guests to stop at the village for something to eat. We walked on, across large Balante rice fields. Cabral, a graduate agronomist, explained how skillfully and painstakingly the plantations were being cultivated. "The earth is very good here," he said. "Geographers like Gouru have always talked about the laterization of African soil. It's as though people were supposed to believe in the inevitable inferiority of both the African and his soil. But he was just generalizing: I know plenty of African countries where the soil is perfectly good."

We canoed across a small inlet of the river. A group of children came over to greet us, and we talked a bit with them. They had not yet learned to read. "It's been at least two years since the Portuguese left," said Cabral, "but because we don't have enough cadres, we haven't been able to do the necessary work of increasing food production and building a school in every village. Some agronomists the Party sent to study abroad are coming back this year, and we're going to train a new batch of teachers in the interior. There's a lot to be done."

We set off again. In the distance we could hear the thud of gunfire. We were to find out later that a skirmish had taken place on the road between Olosato and Bissora, near a bridge that the guerrillas had destroyed and that the Portuguese were doing their best to repair before the start of the rainy season. As we walked on, the forest became thicker. At 9 A.M., after an eight-hour march, we came to the Maké base and were welcomed by Chico, the political commissar for the northern interregion, a well-built fellow with an intelligent, cheerful look. He wore a clean uniform that had no military rank.

A mass of densely packed trees sheltered the clearing where the base was situated. In the middle of a circle thirty yards in diameter there was a central cabin, itself circular and easily capable of holding about fifteen people. It was covered with grass and surrounded by a very sturdy wall woven of banana leaves. The furniture consisted of two wooden tables and two wicker chairs. Fifteen yards or so away stood four smaller cabins, each of which had two wooden beds with grass mattresses and one acetylene lamp. Next to each cabin there was a circular screen of wickerwork and leaves, as well as a large wash basin on a table made of branches. Complete toilet facilities had been set up further away.

After sleeping for three hours and taking a shower, we ate a meal in the central cabin. Plates and glasses had been set on a plastic tablecloth. We had chicken with rice and palm-cabbage oil. Amilcar reached into his bag and took out a bottle of Bacardi rum that Fidel Castro had given him at the Tricontinental Conference as a present for the fighting men. Our waitresses were a group of lively student nurses between the ages of twelve and fifteen who appeared quite attractive in their *boubous*.[1] Cabral chatted and joked with them.

We went to see the camp proper, three hundred yards away behind a clump of trees. On the way, we passed the kitchen, which had been set up under the protection of a giant baobab tree. The fighters' daily meals were cooked over two fireplaces. (The flames were extinguished at the first sign of an air raid.) The food was mainly rice and was served in large pots or enamel pans; the water was drawn from relatively clear springs and kept in big gourds. We came into a clearing and saw about fifty teenage girls, student nurses who had also been to regular school. With them were some forty FARP men in khaki uniforms and plastic sandals, all armed with submachine guns. They were lined up in four rows. Four bazookas, two heavy machine guns, and a mortar were lying in front of them. A hundred guerrillas, equipped with rifles, were standing at attention beside the regular army men. The fighting men were mostly very young, roughly between seventeen and twenty-five.

The camp was a spacious, well-sheltered cabin where the FARP men slept on straw mattresses. The guerrillas had come from their own villages, which were all nearby. Further back was a cabin for the student nurses. Everyone observed complete silence as Amilcar Cabral walked up to talk to the troops. Throughout his speech, we could hear heavy guns in the distance.

"Comrades,

"I have already been to Maké; I have already seen quite a few of you. I am happy to be with you again and to find new faces. To be with a brother again is always a great pleasure, but here we are more than brothers. Two brothers may take different roads. We, members of the Party and fighters for our people, do not have two roads to follow, but one only: the road that leads to freedom and progress for our people.

"In our Party we have sworn to give our lives for the liberation of our people and the building of our country. For this reason we must have a clear picture of the struggle and its difficulties. Girls, women, *homem grande*—you are all sons and daughters of

---

[1] A loose, chemise-like dress worn by women in tropical Africa. (Translators' note.)

the people, and each of you must understand why we are fighting. It is time to put an end to the suffering caused by colonialism—but we must also put an end to the backwardness of our people. There is no point to our struggle if our only goal is to drive out the Portuguese. We want to drive them out, but we are also struggling to end the exploitation of our people, both by whites and by blacks.

"As far as we are concerned, no one has the right to exploit labor. We don't want women and children to continue living in fear. We want all the men and women in our country to be respected. We want to drive out the Portuguese and build. This work cannot be done by one person alone: it must be done by everybody, and, most especially, by those who understand the meaning of their actions. The people must work. A country in which everybody has a chance to work is a prosperous country, for work is what enables us to make progress. Every man and woman must learn that work is their first duty, and that all the workers in the country are useful to the cause. I don't mean just the work of intellectuals or engineers; the jobs done by nurses, carpenters, and mechanics are also very important, but as we see it, tilling the soil is the most important job of all.

"The country that we want to build is a country where people will work. Perhaps you're thinking to yourself: we've been working a long time and we have nothing to show for it. But you were working for the chiefs and the Portuguese. We're going to recover our whole country and work hard in it, but the beneficiaries of this work will be the workers themselves. We are fighting for justice; the product of labor must not be stolen. The only one more valuable than a worker is the one who works even harder. We are already in command in our country. But it means nothing to be in command if we lack schools and hospitals and if we don't manage to change living conditions in the rural areas—for in Guinea the rural areas are crucial. You must not think that we are already free. We are still at war. Of course, we have schools, nurses, and medical stations. We can already hold our heads high because of what the Party has helped us to do and because of what we have done by ourselves. We want our own labor to provide for all of the country's needs: that is what I was anxious to tell you. You already knew it but it's good for you to hear it again. No one, including the leaders and myself, must forget this. A man must have a clear understanding of the struggle at all times.

"The armed struggle is spreading out all over our country. But in the liberated regions some zones are peaceful, while in others fighting takes place every day. This is not right. If ten of us go to the rice paddies and spend a whole day doing the work of eight men, we have no reason to be pleased with ourselves. The same thing applies to the struggle. There are ten of us and we fight like eight. I've talked about this to Oswaldo and Chico. They told me our weapons were inadequate. I say that what is done with them is inadequate. We can always do more. Some people get used to war, and when that happens they're through. They load their rifles and go for a walk. They hear a motor on the river and don't use their bazooka—and the Portuguese boats get through. Once again, I say that we can do more. The Portuguese must be thrown out. I want to make one thing clear: we simply cannot allow the Portuguese boats to get through any more. I am going to talk about this a little later with your Party leaders, and all of us here will talk some more about it, too.

"You must understand that the leader doesn't have to be there in order for you to do your work. I have just come back from Boe— like some of the other Party leaders I have to move around a lot to see how our struggle is developing. Men and women worthy of the name don't need to be urged to perform their duty. They do it by themselves. Otherwise, what's the difference between them and a donkey who won't go forward unless he's driven? I can't be everywhere at once and you shouldn't always be waiting for orders. Oswaldo and Chico don't have to tell you what needs to be done. We must be aware of the job and then do it. Every struggle plods on step by step, but there comes a time to carry it through to the end. Things are uneasy in our Africa: Many peoples had hoped to manage their own affairs, but the colonialists who were leaving are now coming back. Having an African government doesn't mean that one is master of one's destiny. First our work and our wealth have to belong to us—to the people who work to create this wealth. There are others besides the Portuguese who don't want us to be masters in our own land. Once we are independent, they don't want us to be in charge. *They* want to be the leaders. But we're not going to let that happen to us. This is why we must defeat the Portuguese, for the others are their allies. Our Party leadership is strong and resolute, we have weapons, and the people are with us. We have everything we need to get rid of the Portuguese.

"The armed struggle is very important, but the most important thing of all is an understanding of our people's situation. Our people support the armed struggle. We must assure them that those who bear arms are sons of the people and that arms are no better than the tools of labor. Between one man carrying a gun and another carrying a tool, the more important of the two is the man with the tool. We've taken up arms to defeat the Portuguese, but the whole point of driving out the Portuguese is to defend the man with the tool. Teachers are important too. We can wage the struggle and win the war. But if, once we have our country back again, our people are unable to read and write, we will still have achieved nothing. I don't mean that those with an education are more important than the others; the entire people must learn how to read. They must learn how to read so they won't be deceived any longer. I do not speak of being deceived by the Portuguese. We no longer have anything to say to the colonialists. Our dialogue with the Portuguese is the armed struggle. We can already bear arms and speak freely in our country. Our victory is certain, but our struggle isn't really worthwhile unless we respect the people and unless we make it possible for girls like our nurses to be properly brought up and respected. Our struggle is meaningless unless the people are not afraid of those who carry the guns. Our weapons are for use against the Portuguese and not against the people. We will win if everyone performs his duty fearlessly and with understanding. Our struggle will be triumphant if each of us understands that being a Party militant involves certain duties. Our struggle is hard. Our people say, 'Even eating is hard.' We must go on because nothing can stop our people's struggle. But one thing is even more important: we want every son of our land to acquire genuine political awareness. It's up to the Party militants and most especially their leaders to set an example.

"This year the Party will be ten years old. It's still a child, but we have already done a good deal. We've organized the people, we've armed ourselves, and we're going to defeat the colonialists, who used to be stronger than we were. Our Party isn't made up of one man or of its leaders. Many people think that I am the Party: there are others who think that Chico or Oswaldo are the Party. The Party is all those who understand the objectives of our struggle. And many do understand. This is why the Portuguese, the friends of the Portuguese, and even certain Africans want to destroy our Party. All these enemies won't be able to destroy our Party: they simply can't do it. Who can destroy our Party? Only we ourselves can, by our own acts. Every day we must ask ourselves whether what we are doing could endanger the Party. Those who help the Portuguese, of course, they are our enemies—we arrest them and kill them. But the destructive people in our own midst are even more dangerous.

"I am happy to see that your girls' organization is here today. Women belong in school, in the militia, and in village government. I hope you will have the courage and good health to carry the fight against the Portuguese through to the end. We may receive medicine, weapons, and all sorts of things, but nobody can send us crates full of courage. Supplying that is our own job. It was thanks to our courage that we were able to start the struggle, but we're going to need even more courage to win it. Tomorrow, our children will be proud not only of their freedom but also of the new foundations we have laid. Work well, comrades."

Oswaldo, the Party man in charge of military affairs, came forward and said, "We can make the following guarantee: if we receive more weapons, there will be men to use them."

The men stood at attention and presented arms. A green, yellow, and red flag was unfolded. The girls sang the national anthem. Cabral introduced the MPLA comrade and explained the common struggle against Portuguese colonialism in Angola and Mozambique. "Like us," he said, "they are fighting a war to win their independence and to become free men. This is comrade José Mendes, from the Popular Movement for the Liberation of Angola. At present he is one of the senior military officers in the Cabinda *maquis*." Then Cabral explained that some Europeans supported the struggle, even though they came from colonialist countries.

"A revolution is dead when it has no friends in the outside world," he said.

That afternoon some village leaders arrived to greet Cabral. They were wearing the PAIGC badge on their caps. Some of them already knew him; others were meeting him for the first time; most of them had walked four or five hours to reach the camp. They had come to explain problems in their villages, problems concerning livestock, and the harvest and distribution of rice. We were in the central cabin. In a drawer of the table that served as a bookcase, there were a few issues of the newspaper *Le Monde*. Next to them lay several books for the use of the cadres: *The Resistance Will Triumph*, from the Hanoi Foreign Language Press; *Guerrilla Warfare*, by Che Guevara; the *Military Writings* of Mao Tse-tung; and a special issue of *Partisans* devoted to Africa.

About fifteen politico-military cadres from the surrounding zones arrived at the Maké base. All of them were young, between twenty-five and thirty. Their meeting with Cabral, which they intended to tape-record, was devoted to cadre coordination: the topics for discussion were the record for the past few months and the program for the approaching rainy season.

Accompanied by half a dozen guerrilla fighters, we went to visit a Mandingo village located about seven miles from the base. Among our group were Antonio Bana, who spoke Balante and Mandingo, and another interpreter. After an hour's walk through the forest, we stopped near a clear spring where some half-naked little girls were washing laundry. They knew the guerrilla fighters and joked with them.

The Mandingo villagers welcomed us as though they had been expecting our arrival. We gathered inside a small circular area surrounded by several cabins. Some mats had been placed on the ground and about thirty peasants sat down on them. A few of the peasants were in their thirties, but most of them were in their fifties or sixties. (They wore multicolored clothing in which an indigo-blue was especially striking. Only the chief wore a large *boubou*.) When Bissadjar, the village in which they had been living until 1964, was destroyed by bombings, they had decided to take shelter here in the forest, where they would be under the immediate protection of the guerrilla fighters.

Some women came with their little children and remained standing, apart from the men, while a group of inquisitive boys gathered at a distance to observe the proceedings. We were given some salt and some cola as welcoming gifts, and an old woman presented us with a chicken.

This had once been a large village, but the war had forced its breakup into smaller ones. There were thirty families here. The grown men were out in the fields because the rainy season was about to begin and the fields had to be prepared for the rice crop. Most of the men seated across from us were *homem grandes*. Ten young men from the thirty families had joined the guerrilla fighters, and from time to time they came home to visit their relatives. The village had a total population of about 130, with four or five people living in each cabin. Everybody ate together in the place where we were now sitting. The village chief was already chief under the Portuguese, but he made contact with the Party in 1962 and then began to work against the Portuguese. Everyone stopped talking when he got up to tell his story:

"A man couldn't have any self-respect under the Portuguese. Instead of working for themselves, men and women were subjected to forced labor. All we had under the Portuguese was forced labor, taxes, whippings, and canings. We haven't seen any Portuguese around here for two years. Our village was destroyed in 1963. They took away the livestock before that.

"The Party protects us now. We work for our own benefit, and we also give rice to the fighting men because they're like our own flesh and blood. We need quite a few things. We don't have any more money—so we just don't spend it! Anyway, there hasn't been anything to buy for two years. We could use some cloth to make clothes with. This year the Party's going to set up people's stores and we'll be able to exchange rice and groundnuts for cloth. But even with the hardships and the war, we're still better off than we were under the Portuguese. Besides the head tax, we used to have all kinds of taxes. For instance, sometimes the post commanders would come and show movies glorifying the Portuguese.

Well, you had to pay to see these movies, and even if you didn't go, they made you pay anyway. The situation was unbearable. We had some livestock—all the villagers want to have livestock—but you couldn't say that it was really ours. Every so often the Portuguese came, took what they wanted, and paid what they wanted for it—and they always paid very little.

"If you had seen us under the Portuguese, you would have known immediately that we weren't happy. We had no control over our goods or our work, and we had to cater to the whims of the administrators. We have to put up with a great deal now because of the war, but we also know that everything that's happening is for our own benefit. We can do whatever we want with what little we have. That's why we're satisfied in spite of the hardships. Living under colonialism is like being drunk: well, we're healthy now. The peasants are hoping that their hardships will come to an end and that they'll enjoy a better life after the victory's been won."

The village chief sat down. At our request, a *homem grande* got up to speak. Antonio Bana told him he could remain seated while giving his talk if he preferred to do so. The old man sat down again and said:

"I used to work in the fields during the rainy season while we were still under the Portuguese. During the dry season I worked as an itinerant peddler, selling cola and tobacco for money. We haven't got any more money here now. There are thirteen of us in my family. I have three wives and eight children—four daughters and four sons. Three of my daughters are married, and the other one lives with me. My sons are living with me, too: the oldest is on the Party committee. Things were very bad under the Portuguese, but even now, we still have to put up with many hardships. Since we don't have any money, we can't buy anything. That's why we need people's stores. There hasn't been any trade here for two years. After the struggle's over, and the Portuguese are no longer around to take advantage of us, we'll be well off. We'll be able to buy whatever we want, and whatever we have will really belong to us."

The chief and the *homem grande* had spoken in Mandingo. Now a young man got up to say a few words in Creole:

"Nobody died when our village was bombed because we heard the planes coming and were able to hide from them. But all the cabins burned to the ground. One member of our village was killed while making some purchases. The Portuguese accused him of giving supplies to the *bandoleiros*. No one wants to go back to the village. We're here now, and we've started to get the fields in shape for the rain.

"This is the way we work: during the rainy season, we form teams of five comrades each. Everyone has his own field, but we till all the soil communally, and we eat together, too. We own our tools and harvest the crop individually."

The village had a Party committee composed of three men and three women. (During the speeches, the women had sat down.) Two of the men on the committee were absent. The third, who could not have been more than thirty, got up to speak:

"The village committee's duties are highly varied. In the long run, every problem that comes up has to be settled by the committee. If we have a problem we can't solve, we take it to the regional representative for political affairs. What kinds of problems do we take care of? We might have to take care of transporting an arms shipment, for example. In this case, the Party leaders would notify the committee; the committee would tell the village what had to be done and then select men to do the job, preferably on a volunteer basis. The committee supervises the husking of the fighters' rice crop because we know that the fighters are waging the people's struggle. The fighters defend the village against the Portuguese. Now the Portuguese don't come around any longer. We still have a bit of livestock, and we've taken it to a place where it will be better protected. The young people are in charge of feeding it and caring for it."

While the committee member's little speech was still going on, the village chief, who was an *almamo* (religious leader) as well, performed his ablutions, knelt down on a mat, and began to say his prayers. The other *homem grandes* went on listening and smoking their clay pipes.

"What are the committee's political duties?"

"We hold meetings to explain our fight for freedom. We tell the people that there will be no more racial or sexual discrimination, and that we'll all be brothers."

"Do you all agree?"

"Yes."

"Do you produce a lot?"

"We have millet, corn, *fonio*, sorghum, and above all rice. There's enough to go round. Sometimes we have beef. We also hunt and fish, and we used to raise chickens."

"What does the Party mean to the village?"

"When a group of people get together with a single objective in mind, that makes a Party. The Party's not a person, it's a thing. We're all after the same end. If you're wondering why we're in this war, it's because we want to get the Portuguese off our backs so everybody can work and be happy."

After a little coaxing, the oldest woman on the committee agreed to make a few remarks. She said: "I'm in the Party because the Party's going to help us win our freedom, and then we'll be able to work in peace. We women take part in meetings and express our opinions freely. The aim of everyone here is mutual understanding. If two people have a disagreement, then the committee has to settle their problem. The men and women here think and act as one person, and their opinions are respected by all the committee members. As for our problems, well, we don't have a general store, and we need to buy loin-cloths, scarves, and material for clothes. There aren't any other problems. The struggle goes on and we pray that God will allow us to reach our goals and satisfy our needs."

A *homem grande* got up to ask how agricultural work could be improved during the rainy season. Antonio Bana replied that three agronomists who had been trained abroad would soon be assigned to the northern region. He reminded everyone that production was of prime importance to the struggle, and in introducing José Mendes he talked about the common struggle being waged by the people of Angola and Mozambique.

Toward suppertime, we took a walk around the base. All the fires were out. In the twilight, we could see several groups of fighters squatting around a cooking-pot and eating their rice.

We ate supper with some cadres who had come for work-sessions with Cabral. They had all been in the back country for three or four years. Eight of them were peasants who could not read or write—on-the-spot recruits who were products of the struggle. Four of the cadres were either mechanics or workers from the port of Bissau. Chico and Oswaldo, the highest-ranking officers, came from the petty bourgeoisie. None of the officers worked in his home region. Cabral talked about the *coups d'état* that had taken place in Africa. He discussed the example of Ghana at great length and explained how Nkrumah was largely responsible for his own downfall. He also touched on the role played by Ghana's middle class. Throughout the meal, we could hear the distant thud of field artillery alternating with bursts of automatic fire nearby. The moon seemed almost to have sunk into the livid sky, and the Portuguese must have been firing at random.

"They're just shooting by rote," said Cabral.

When the conference of cadres had ended, Cabral rapidly drew up a communiqué to be sent to all cadres in the north:

"Comrades,

"During three days of intensive work, we discussed the principal problems concerning our mode of life and our struggle in the northern interregion. In addition to providing an overall review of the present situation in Guinea and Cape Verde and of the concrete prospects for our struggle, the cadre conference constitutes a new proof of our Party's strength. As a sequel to the conference just held in the southern interregion, our conference has completed an important task in this stage of our struggle by taking stock of the situation, analyzing our successes and our errors, and settling upon solutions for the problems posed by the evolution of our struggle and by the new requirements of our mode of life.

"In the course of the conference, we studied in depth the various problems related to the various regions and zones of the north —problems of a military and political nature as well as problems relating to the other aspects of our life (production, supply, culture and education, and data on the population). We dealt with the study of these problems, and most especially with the analysis

CONFIDENCIAL
ORDEM DE OPERAÇOES
N° 18/66

Ex N° 4
BCAV 79 ø
BULA
161 øøø MAR 66
C 68 F

OPERAÇAO "ACHEGA"

Referencia: carta 1/50,000 — PELUNDO
Composiçao des Forças: CCAC 1489 (−) + Milicias

1) SITUATION

The enemy continues to make his presence felt in Jol, where he showed great willingness to fight in the N.T. [advance unit] actions that preceded Operation Capim. He has proved to be combat-hardened and well-trained and has made effective use of the weapons he possesses.

Organized in highly mobile groups, he appeared on all routes taken by the N.T.'s and mainly employed light arms. Throughout Operation Capim, he indicated his presence by shooting a few bursts of gunfire in the distance and by laying an ambush near Gel. He fired only three shots in this ambush and then withdrew when confronted with the counterattack of our forces.

2) MISSION

Attempt to localize the enemy's tactical retreat zones and to launch offensive actions against them, in order to liquidate or capture rebel elements and to destroy property or crops. Pay special attention to Mandjak and Feloupe fields.

CAPTURED PORTUGUESE DOCUMENT

of the causes and consequences of our weaknesses and errors, by utilizing the method of constructive criticism and frank self-criticism.

"As a result of the two conferences of cadres, north and south, we have drawn up the enclosed general directives, based on data furnished by the conference of cadres in the north and on decisions reached by the conference. These directives for the northern region are issued in the name of our Party's political bureau.

"Study the following directives carefully, and make the efforts and sacrifices necessary to implement them correctly. I am certain that we shall achieve new and decisive victories against the Portuguese colonial forces and for the progress of our people.

The Secretary-General—A. Cabral"

DIRECTIVES FOR THE NORTHERN INTERREGION[2]

I. *Information about the struggle:*
Fighters, militants, and masses to be kept as well-informed as possible.

II. *Political action:*
a) Intensification of political training;
b) Party security; vigilance; the number of intelligence agents to be increased;
c) political work in enemy territory never to be neglected;
d) Party congress to be prepared for.

III. *Reorganization:*
a) Of regional structure, in accord with the evolution of the struggle;[3]
b) assignment of people to positions of responsibility by Party leadership in accord with the recommendations of the cadre conference;
c) reorganization of zones (after consultation with representatives of the people and the Party's zone committee).[4]

---

[2] The content of these directives is obviously not included here: only the outline and the chapter headings of Cabral's text are given.

[3] See above, pp. 21–27, on the struggle of the PAIGC.

[4] Zonal structure is as follows: a senior officer, a political commissar, commissars for security and the people's militia, for public health, for education and civil status. The same positions exist on the regional and interregional levels. On the zone level, commissars are assigned by the Party leadership.

IV. *Armed struggle:*
- a) Intensification of the struggle;
- b) heavy armament;
- c) development of telecommunications (reinforce hook-ups);
- d) development of army units (FARP); points to be reinforced to be determined according to objectives;
- e) evacuations of Portuguese deserters;
- f) transportation of materiel;
- g) details of top-priority actions to be carried out in the various regions.

V. *Party representation on the northern border, in Casamance.*
VI. *Situation of certain persons holding positions of responsibility: tasks, new functions, dismissals.*

Special emphasis was placed on points IV and V. The PAIGC pays particular attention to political work, which precedes and then complements the armed struggle.

Chico, age twenty-seven, political commissar for the northern interregion, speaks:

"We've held elections for a Party committee in each village of the liberated regions. We call it a *tabanca* [Creole for village] committee. In general, it is composed of three men and three women, and is elected by the village assembly, in other words, by the entire adult population of the village. We explain beforehand the way in which they must get organized, the tasks they have to carry out, and, of course, the basic principles of the Party. Young people are often elected. The old people haven't always been happy to see their places in the village leadership taken over by the young. Almost all our fighters are young, too, of course. But then again, since everybody, old and young, had had enough of the Portuguese, even the old ones who at first dragged their feet finally came around. So anyhow, committee officers are elected by the villagers. We in the Party are consulted, and we decide to support a candidate on the basis of the work he has already accomplished for the Party and of the esteem in which the other peasants hold him. In principle, the peasants' choice is respected. If, in our opinion, they have chosen badly, we leave the candidate in office. We wait for the peasants to realize their mistake by themselves. Naturally, the Party reserves the right to remove those who use their prerogatives in their own interests. We don't want a new chieftainship system. A new committee is elected at the peasants' request; and elections are also held periodically just to avoid what you might call hardening of the arteries.

"The village committee has several tasks. At the present stage, one of the most important is to increase agricultural production, so that there will be plenty of rice for both families and fighters. The fighters also produce rice, millet, etc., but their food is supplied mainly by the village. We've created new collective fields so that the villagers can produce for the fighters. The village committee takes care of supervising and administering the work, and it also takes care of the militia. The militia consists of young people who are not FARP fighters but guerrilla partisans with rifles and no uniforms. They are part of the village's self-defense group. In certain zones, they play an offensive role. They live in the village. The FARP fighters, however, leave the village and are transferred from place to place according to the requirements of the struggle. Obviously, they are volunteers. They join us because of our political work in the villages. This work is done in the local languages. Around here, the village people speak Balante and Mandingo, and a certain number of peasants understand Creole. My own native language is Pepel, but I can't speak it because I always lived in Bissau. I've learned Balante and Mandingo in the course of the struggle.

"Political work means getting people to learn about the Party and explaining why we exist and what we want. We explain what colonialism means. At first, we explain that Guinea isn't Portugal and that we can govern ourselves without the Portuguese taking our livestock, without heavy taxes, and blows, and fear of the Portuguese. We explain that what's happening here isn't an act of God, and that it's already happened in a lot of other countries. We have to show our people that the world doesn't end at their villages. Our problem is to make them understand the present level of the struggle, the fact that the struggle doesn't concern just their village but all of Guinea, and that it's not simply a national but also an international struggle. We have to make them aware that in order to advance, *they* must guarantee the struggle's continuity, *they* must take charge of their own destiny by solving their problems on the village level, developing production, sending their children to school, and holding frequent meetings.

"In actual practice, meetings are regular as long as the Party is present. If the Party is not on the scene, meetings become fewer and farther between and finally stop altogether. Our people are just beginning to be free, and everything can't go on from one day to the next as the Party wishes. But bit by bit, there are signs of progress. In general, village committees meet two or three times a month. Even when it functions imperfectly, the village committee is respected because it's almost always made up of the best elements in the village. Of course, sometimes one of the committee members commits an error. In that case, he is removed. Recently, for instance, one of the neighboring villages had a problem about the rice that had been harvested and set aside for the fighters. One of the committee members appropriated it for his own profit. He was expelled from the committee and someone else was elected to replace him. Depending on production, the villages give the fighters rice, palm-cabbage, corn, millet, and sometimes livestock when there is any available. The population feels protected by those who are doing the fighting. Some villages haven't seen any Portuguese in almost three years. The most difficult problem of all is getting the committee in motion—getting it to do what has to be done, and especially getting it to act much more often on its own initiative.

"We also have to give the fighters political training. The essential principle is that no difference must be created between the fighters and the people for whom they're fighting. We explain to them that our struggle is directed neither against the Portuguese people nor against white skin, that our enemies are all those opposed to our country's freedom, that there are Portuguese who are for us and Africans who serve the Portuguese, and that our weapons don't come from Africa but from countries where the people don't have black skin. Military training takes place at the same time as political training. We teach weaponry and the general principles of guerrilla warfare. But above all, there is actual field combat. There's no precise training-period for a fighter: it's always coordinated with his concrete participation in combat. Political training, however, never finishes: that's why each unit has a political commissar. We also place great stress on discipline, during and between combat engagements. We're very strict about alcohol and sexual relations.

"We explain to everybody, fighters and villagers alike, that our struggle is being waged not only to drive out the Portuguese but also to build and develop the country; that in order to be free, the people themselves must take charge of the country and that they must be the ones who profit from their labor. We explain that we need bridges, hospitals, and schools, and that tomorrow's construction will be the hardest phase of all. The people will have a new life, but only if they work for it. We have no intention of struggling now and relaxing later, because the things we hope to get won't come to us all by themselves. The outlook for the future is work, before everything else: actually, work should assume top priority starting right now.[5]

"As far as the ethnic problems are concerned, the Party has devoted a lot of effort to them, and it alone could attempt to solve them correctly. These conflicts have just about disappeared in the course of the struggle against the Portuguese. Of course, the Portuguese played the Fulah chiefs against the Party. The PAIGC tried to explain the new situation to the Fulah population by demonstrating that it was in the Portuguese interest to support the chiefs in order to rule over all the rest of us. But there were many who didn't want to understand what we were saying, because they didn't want to lose what they already had. They have been considerably influenced and corrupted by the Portuguese. The Fulah chiefs fled to the cities for protection, and although

---

[5] The day before, when an old man complained about his hardships, Chico had said: "Since the day you were born, how much have you put together to leave your children? You're not going to leave anything, because the Portuguese have taken it all. The only inheritance you can leave your sons is freedom, and that's a great deal, because they can obtain everything else by working."

some Fulah elements joined the Party, others followed the customary chiefs.

"In 1963–64, there came a point at which the armed struggle reached a temporary stage of equilibrium and the Portuguese were using repressive methods to implant fear in the population. We explained that Portuguese colonialism was heaving its last gasps, and we increased our efforts to create a permanent state of insecurity. Since the end of 1964, the struggle on the battlefield has gone in our favor. At that time, certain Fulahs came to ask for the Party's protection. Of course, there are regions that we don't control, like the Balante coastal regions around Bissau, the Fulah highland regions, the Mandjak regions in the center, and the Felupe regions. But it's just a question of time—I mean of getting enough cadres.

"In the present phase of the struggle, the essential task is to make the village committees function properly and to form section committees that will connect five or six villages. We've begun to set these up. According to the size of the villages, each section committee has ten to fifteen members. In addition, there is the necessary work of production. Of course, the major problem is still the armed struggle. We must continue to widen our encirclement of the Portuguese and begin the struggle in regions that have not yet been liberated. In order to begin the struggle in new areas successfully, we have to create a new relationship of forces. The first difficulty is the peasants' fear of Portuguese repression. In the Mandjak regions, where the struggle began about six months ago, the population has stopped frequenting the urban centers and now places itself under the protection of the fighters.

"We must first explain our struggle politically and make a precise study of the regional situation, which may or may not be favorable, depending on circumstances. We send in the FARP only after completing this first task and only if it shows positive results. We prefer to send fighters who were born in the region and who speak its language. The people in charge are Guinean— and that's all that counts.

"After creating a new relationship of forces by virtue of our military action, we have to replace the colonial infrastructure with our own administrative and economic infrastructure, in order to affirm our presence and to take care of the population's elementary needs. That's why the people's stores are important. In the south, they function pretty well. Here, we need more.

"Our struggle has been successful because two years before launching the armed struggle, Amilcar trained hundreds of cadres in Conakry and sent dozens of them to do the work of explanation and mobilization in the villages. When we began the struggle, we didn't have to hide from the Portuguese and the villagers, because the peasants informed us about every move made by the Portuguese troops. Since then, we have always taken precautions to avoid a split between the fighters and the population."

In the Oïo Forest

We left Maké. A six-hour march separated us from Morès, the central base in the north. We soon came to the dense Oïo forest, the nerve-center of the guerrilla forces in the northern part of the country. On the way, we crossed over two beaten paths lined with bushy, evenly planted trees that shaded us comfortably. These were Portuguese roads, one going from Olosato to Bissora and the other from Mansaba to Bissora. This time we marched by daylight. We were divided into three groups of ten men each. At a spot where water had flooded part of the plain, we waded jokingly through the mud and water. From time to time, we sank in up to our knees, and our soaking shoes made a squeaky sound that lent a jaunty rhythm to the column's march. Fidelis, a cadre who had come with us from Dakar, lost one of his sandals as he was wading through the water, and was unable to find it. Turning to the guerrillas, he asked:

"Who wears size 9 shoes here?"

"I do," answered a voice.

"Let me have your shoes."

"I'm not wearing any," answered the voice.

It was so hot that we were dry when we arrived at Morès. It is the oldest base in the north. The vegetation there is very thick. The people at the base moved about over narrow paths that were lined with trees and bushes. With its various dependencies—a school, a country hospital, dormitories, and kitchens—the camp was almost one mile in diameter. When we arrived, some soldiers on sentry duty stood at attention and saluted Cabral. As at Maké, there were individual cabins for temporary guests, as well as a large cabin for assemblies and a cabin for the camp's two surgeons. The men lived in two spacious, well-protected billets. They slept on straw mats. The camp was guarded all around by groups spread out over a radius of three miles. The fighters wore regulation uniforms and were just as young as their comrades at Maké. They had a large supply of weapons and kept them in good repair. These included field artillery pieces, several types of bazookas that had come from various sources, and heavy and light machine guns. Cabral would later review two hundred FARP fighters, each of whom was armed with a submachine gun. The guerrillas who came to report at the base were armed with rifles.

The first in a series of ten arterial bombardments that were to occur over the next two weeks took place at noon, shortly after our arrival. Three of these bombings were to be particularly violent and close to our positions. The attacks came in response to the unremitting guerrilla actions that had been launched against Portuguese camps and posts twenty-four hours after Cabral's arrival. At the start of this first bombing, we heard a dull noise, at which the fighters immediately pricked up their ears. As the noise grew louder, the order was given to spread out in the forest and hide there. There were no trenches or shelters.

Three airplanes approached and were soon flying overhead. According to general estimates, they were flying at an approximate altitude of 4,500–6,000 feet. One of the planes was an American B-26; the other two were West German Fiat P.V.2.[6] Now they

_____

[6] Portugal is a member of NATO. An article by J. Amalric in *Le Monde* of October 15, 1966, mentions the illegal sale of American bombers to Portugal. In the course of a sensational trial, Messrs. Henri de Montmarin and John Hawke were accused of "violating U.S. law by illegally transporting seven B-26 bombers from American territory, for the purpose of delivering them to Portugal." According to Hawke, ". . . the American government did not give its official consent to export the bombers because it was bound by its agreement not to supply Portugal with offensive weapons for her struggle against the Afri-

turned around and we heard the heavy thud of bombs and the crackling of machine guns as the planes went into a momentary dive without really lowering their altitude. Three planes had been shot down the year before during the rainy season because they were flying below 3,000 feet. Lying flat, we made sure that the metal of our weapons would not reflect the glaring sunlight. The raid lasted about half an hour. Absolute silence reigned in the forest: we heard only the hum of the airplanes and the heavy sound of falling bombs.

That afternoon we heard that their fire had come within two and a half miles of the camp, near a former base where they had noticed smoke: some women were making soap with ashes. We returned to the base with two doctors. The country hospital was extremely simple. It consisted of a small enclosure with a wooden operating table; another table for general examinations, with medical instruments in stainless steel boxes; one cabin for the wounded, one for the sick; and, finally, a walled-in cabin holding about 450 pounds of various medical supplies needed to cope with the problems that arise in the back country. The wounded were lying on straw mats. There were four civilians and two soldiers. They had all been hit by bomb fragments—in the arms, legs, and shoulder. They had been operated on without anesthetic, because none was available at the time. One of them had a broken wrist. He was treated and recovered the use of his hand, but he would eventually need surgery to break the bone again and then reset it. "That's not our job," said one of the doctors. "Here, we close things up; we don't open them." In a few days, the civilians would be allowed to return to their villages, and the soldiers would be able to resume combat duty.

In general, the patients had either malaria or intestinal parasites, according to the diagnosis of our two surgeons, who had been trained abroad and had come to Morès several months earlier.

---

can nationalists; but the Central Intelligence Agency arranged the whole deal." The trial ended with a dismissal of charges.

Portugal is said to have received nearly 10,000 automatic weapons from West Germany. In 1965, despite a protest from the Canadian government, West Germany delivered sixty fighter planes made in Canada to the Salazar government.

Their examinations of the population had revealed vitamin-B deficiency in almost every case, caused by the absence of vegetables in a diet based almost exclusively on rice and starches. There were very few cases of leprosy, tuberculosis, or syphilis, but the doctors almost always found intestinal parasites, malaria, dermatitis (caused by friction and lack of proper hygiene), and *yahya*, or *matacanca*, a type of vermin that lodges in the sole of the foot and eats away the epidermis. In general, the population and the troops were considered to be in reasonably good health. The women were more reticent about having medical examinations than the men, especially among the Islamized elements of the population, but they had gradually begun to come on their own initiative, often in small groups.

Armed sentries once more took up their guard posts along the paths leading to and from the camp. The sounds of renewed activity broke the heavy silence observed during the bombardment. A Portuguese deserter who had come to the camp a week before was listening to *fados* [folksongs] broadcast by Radio Bissau on a transistor that someone had given him for his entertainment. In the kitchen, where both men and women were busy at work, four low fires had been rekindled to cook the rice. A green parrot was perched silently on a branch. There were large tins of apricots (with Gevrey-Chambertin and Côte d'Or labels) and Maggi seasoning, as well as supplies of rice and manioc. Live chickens were being kept in wicker baskets, two small goats had been fastened to a rope, and a piglet was running around loose.

Interviews with fighters

Armando Joaquim Soto Amado, age twenty-one:
"I've been at this base for nearly a year. I used to be at Fulador, not far from the Guinean border. I've been a guerrilla for two and a half years; before that I was a joiner's assistant in the Texeira Diniz factory in Bissau. I didn't earn much as an apprentice—my salary came to 150 escudos a month. All my earnings went for food. I lived at my brother's in the suburbs. Now he's gone back to the family in the interior. My father knew how to read and owned a plot of land. He died when we were little. He

left us a small rice field and some fruit trees. My brother isn't participating in the struggle. I was first arrested because they suspected me of subversive activities. I spent a month and a half in prison. Then they gave me a sort of conditional release by sending me to an administrative post in the interior. I worked as a houseboy for the head of the post. They didn't pay me anything, and I ran away. So the Portuguese took my uncle and killed him.

"I'm fighting to liberate my country so that it will become what we want it to be: a free country with social justice.

"The Party has taught me how to fight and how to wage the struggle against Portuguese domination. When I came to my first base, I received military and political training and they gave me my own weapon. Our training is never really over—we're always learning something new. I took part in operations like ambushes, patrols, and regular battles all through 1964. Now I'm no longer a guerrilla. I belong to the FARP.

"The political commissar of our group accompanies us when we go into combat. Before the start of the attack, he explains the reasons for our battle. The military commander often tells us to respect the political commissar as the most important individual in the group. We have many daily duties at the base. In addition to patrols and military training, we have to be prepared for all sorts of tasks that come up unexpectedly. The rest of the time, I relax when I can; I do my laundry in order to pass inspection; and I study reading and writing. Some of the others took up studying and then dropped it, but I'm trying to continue. There are twenty-three of us in my group: twenty troops like me, two political commissars, and one group leader. I'm responsible for handling the machine gun. It's a very fine one—the clip holds a hundred bullets. We don't always eat very well, but we can't complain. After all, we're in the middle of the struggle, and besides, there's plenty of fruit everywhere.

"I speak Pepel and Creole. I belong to the same religion as my father, my grandfather, and their ancestors. I used to practice it before the start of the struggle, and although I don't practice any longer, I still believe. God is called 'Iran.' I brought God's name with me when I entered the struggle. When I go into battle, I ask Iran to keep me from being killed, so I have both

God and my weapon on my side. But if someone dies, his soul continues to live. I'm not immortal, and when it's time for me to die, I'll die. It doesn't bother me. It doesn't make me happy or sad: there's nothing I can do about it.

"Right now I'm busy with the struggle. Marriage will have to wait until the struggle's over. As long as my wife's Guinean, I don't care about the tribe she comes from. I didn't think that way before. I respected the law of the group. But the Party taught me otherwise, and now I think the Party's right. We have all kinds of people in the struggle—Pepels, Mandjaks, Balantes, etc. My wife will be a participant in the struggle."

Tombon Seidi, age sixteen:

"My parents live in one of the neighboring villages. Their language is Mandingo. They agreed to let me come into the forest. My mother has a position of responsibility in the Party. My father grows groundnuts, rice, and corn. He has his own land. I began to take part in the struggle a year ago, not far from this base. I went through military training, and in six months of active duty I've been in combat nine times. I left the guerrillas a month ago, and I'm now in the FARP. I'm not wearing my uniform today because it's torn. We're fighting against the Portuguese so they'll go away. We're going to get rid of them. They beat our parents and wore them out with hard work. Our parents had to do too much work for nothing. They got robbed every time they sold their produce to the Portuguese. And the head tax was just too high.

"You want to know what I'd like to do after we get our independence? [Tombon reflected at length before answering.] I want to be a soldier so I can protect and defend my country."

Ireño do Nascimiento Lopes, leader, age twenty-five:

"Here in the north, the struggle has made good progress. It would be far less advanced than it is if the people hadn't given us the support we needed. We began the struggle in 1963, with only three weapons for each base. There was no shortage of volunteers—on the contrary—but we were short of weapons. Thanks to the courage of our fighters and to the example set by Oswaldo, we overcame these difficulties. During this period, the Portuguese did all they could to nip us in the bud. But we survived and even gained ground. We're going to keep on gaining until we drive the Portuguese out.

"I became involved in the struggle in 1962. Long before that I already knew that other African countries had become independent, and that Guinea wasn't one of them. Then the Party came along, and when I found out about the Party, I tried to make contact with it. The Party members I met said they wanted our people and our country to be free. So I joined up. My other comrades managed to reach Conakry, where they enrolled in the cadre training courses, but I was arrested by the PIDE [Portuguese political police] and was sent to battalion No. 3-56 in the Portuguese camp at Castillo for a month. After that, I spent five months in the PIDE's prison in Bissau. I was subjected to corporal punishment and endured every kind of humiliation. They tied me to a rope like an ox and tortured me in every possible way. Afterward they released me. I went to look for the president of our organization because I'd made up my mind to join Oswaldo, who was in the back country somewhere near Morès. Twelve of us left Bissau secretly at about 6 A.M. We took a break for several hours and then went on to Morès. Since I was carrying a message from Chairman Rafael Barbosa to the secretary-general of the PAIGC, I left for the south, walking all the way to the Guinean border, and caught up with Amilcar Cabral in Conakry. I remembered all the suffering I underwent in prison, and I returned to the struggle with feelings of deep hatred for the Portuguese. I swore to kill every Portuguese I saw as soon as I could get hold of a gun. I took Cabral's courses in Conakry and they enabled me to see things with an open mind. The Party gave me a clear idea of the reasons for the struggle and taught me to distinguish between those Portuguese who are our friends and those who are our enemies. For instance, I've gotten very friendly with some of the Portuguese deserters. We've eaten meals together and have had a chance to talk things over. After the courses gave me a political understanding of our struggle, I was permitted to go home and assume military duties in the back country."

José Augusto Texeira Mourao, Portuguese deserter, age twenty-one:

(Mourao had been at Morès for about a week and a half. He was not the first of his kind. Occasional deserters[7] had been turning themselves in since 1963, usually after reading a Party leaflet or coming in contact with a PAIGC militant. Most of them had political motives. The Party evacuates them to Senegal or Guinea and then to the destination of their choice. They often go to Algiers, where they join the Portuguese Liberation Front, FPLN. This latest arrival, twenty-one years old, was tall and thin and had light brown hair. He walked back and forth in the center of camp, carrying his transistor. He had not deserted for political reasons.)

"I deserted because they treated us too roughly. If you make a small mistake, you get beaten, especially by the head corporal; then they put you in jail and reduce your rations. After serving two months in Portugal, I was in Bissau for six months. Nobody was happy at the thought of coming here, but the officers kept driving us on. A hitch lasts 24, 28, and sometimes 30 months.[8] Afterward they sent me to the interior, to an outpost in Buba that had 500 men. I ended up in Biambi, where there were 220 of us. The camp was fortified. In daytime they send a few men outside, but never very far from the camp. Aside from fatigue duty, the men play basketball and cards. At night they rotate on guard. The watchtowers are lit and you can see for more than 300 yards. You wait for the attack to come, and that puts you on edge. Sometimes three attacks come in one night, and that really puts you on edge. Other times, nothing happens, and that puts you even more on edge. At least it's quiet here.

"My father works in a tile factory. I went to school until I was eleven and started working in Porto when I was fourteen. I got called up in 1964. When we were stationed in Bissau, we used to patrol all around the outskirts, but we never ran into the enemy. The food was bad all the time. I griped about its poor quality,

---

[7] See, for example, "Deux déserteurs portuguais parlent," *Révolution Africaine*, No. 49, January 2, 1964.

[8] In December 1966, the length of military service was increased to four years.

and because of that the head corporal gave me twenty days in the stockade. Then they transferred me to posts in the interior—Buba, N'Gore, Binar, and finally Biambi, where I deserted. On a routine day, we'd get up at seven, wash up, assemble for roll call, and eat breakfast. Then we had fatigue duty. It was boring and the work was rough—I still have calluses from it. After supper, we'd clean up, have our weapons inspected, and receive our assignments for guard duty. The sentries are on two-hour shifts, and lights-out is at nine-thirty.

"The men are bored. They don't have anything to do and they aren't even allowed to gripe. Except for a few guys who don't seem to mind it too much, most of the men are really unhappy. If someone starts making trouble, they send him to a post way off in the sticks. The officers know damn well that the guerrillas are strong. They think that because the guerrillas keep on getting more and more men to fight for them, we have to kill every one we catch. They tell us that if we're taken prisoner, we'll have our heads cut off. That convinces our men not to desert. When I deserted, I didn't know the Party was in this area.

"In May, three different artillery attacks were launched against our camp. Shortly before my arrival at Biambi, four men and a captain died in an ambush. The other camps are attacked frequently too. At Biambi, we used to go for a daily swim in the river just outside the camp. Twelve days ago, when everybody else was in the water, I left my weapon near a thicket and went over the hill. I also had six hand grenades on me—four of them offensive and two defensive. That was on May 16. On the seventeenth I reached a Balante village. The villagers weren't frightened except when they saw my grenades, which I took out and put on the ground. After that they were very nice to me. They gave me something to eat and went to inform the guerrillas, who came for me a few hours later. I've been getting good treatment and good food ever since."

That morning, while a group of Portuguese planes was flying over Mores on its way to bomb targets elsewhere, Cabral suggested a visit to the schoolchildren and the troops. We went off with Titina, the camp nurse. She wore an FARP uniform and carried a rifle. The schoolchildren sat in orderly fashion on mats that they had spread out on the ground next to their cabins. There were twenty girls in a group of 120, and they sat with the boys. All wore FARP uniforms. When we first arrived, the children stood at attention.

Amilcar was sitting on a stool, with José Mendes and Titina next to him. He first introduced Mendes and explained that Guinea was not alone in its struggle but that the other Portuguese colonies of Angola, Mozambique, and São Tomé were also fighting for their independence. "You are the future," he said. "We are waging this struggle to make you free. But you won't be doing enough if you simply accept your freedom without developing a genuine political awareness of what it means. This is why you must take your studies very seriously, for the most important resources a country can have are the men and women who live in it—if they treat each other as equals. For instance, look at Titina who's standing here next to me. She's a PAIGC cadre and a qualified nurse. Men and women must have the same rights and the same duties, and you must understand this because you will be the Party of tomorrow. What about your village committee—are there any women on it?"

Everybody answered: "Yes!"

"And who here is on the committee?" asked Cabral.

Four boys and two girls, all about twelve years old, stepped up and gave a brief account of the work they did as leaders.

"Now, does anybody have any questions?" asked Amilcar.

A boy named Djassi rose from his seat and began by welcoming the Party's secretary-general with a long series of compliments.

Amilcar interrupted him: "That's not a question. Ask me questions—about the struggle."

A girl spoke up: "Here we get up early every day and go straight to work. What about our comrades at school in Conakry?"

"They work, too," said Amilcar. "They've made a tape-recording for you, and you'll have a chance to hear it shortly."

Someone else asked: "What about the wounded fighters that we evacuated? Have they recovered yet?"

Cabral gave news of the wounded men. Then he talked about fresh medical supplies that had arrived from various countries and about international solidarity.

Titina got up and asked if anybody was in charge of public health. She received a negative reply and said, "Well, that has to be taken care of. You can elect some people right now. Their job will be to hold a personal hygiene inspection every morning." The schoolchildren quickly voted in a public health committee. They were clearly used to living as a group and handling organizational matters for themselves.

"I've brought you a present," said Amilcar, as he took a large, multicolored rubber ball out of his bag and tossed it in the center of the group. Everyone applauded.

"Work is the most important thing of all," said Cabral, "far more important than play. It's urgent that we have hospitals and schools for everyone between the ages of seven and fifteen. We'll have to work to get them. Man's labor—and by that I mean the labor of men and women—produces all the good things in the world. In our national anthem, there's a line that says: 'We will build peace and progress.' Well, work is the only way to go about building progress. Here in Africa we're very fond of dancing and playing the tom-tom, and that's fine. But we also have to work. I've just come back from Cuba, where they do a lot of dancing and singing, but they work, too. What's our favorite sport here in Guinea?"

"The struggle!" answered a few of the boys.

"That's right, the struggle," said Cabral. "And work is man's most important struggle. You can be a good dancer, a good athlete, and a good worker all at the same time."

Cabral took out the tape recorder and played the message from the pupils in the Conakry pilot school. They spoke about their studies and their daily activities. Then they sang a song, and our group joined in with them.

A young boy raised his hand and wanted to know if he could ask the Angolan comrade a question. His question was: "What's the struggle like in Angola?"

José Mendes explained the particular problems of the struggle in Angola and talked about guerrilla action there. He said that the population was war-weary.

Another boy, who couldn't have been much older than ten, raised his hand and said: "The comrade said that people in Angola were tired because the struggle was hard. Well, we think the struggle's hard, too, but we don't want to rest, and we can't let ourselves get tired, because afterward we'll be independent."

"Are there any other questions?" asked Amilcar.

A boy said: "What about the kids over in Angola? Are they brave? Here, we do all we can to encourage the fighters, and they're sometimes our parents or our relatives. That makes them even braver, and . . ."

Amilcar cut him off. "You're not asking a question—you're making a speech." The children laughed. Then he asked: "Does anyone have a question for the Frenchman?"

At first no one answered him. Finally a little girl raised her hand and said: "Let him ask us questions."

I asked: "If you had a technical school where you could learn manual trades, would anyone volunteer to study there?"

The question was translated, but no one raised his hand. Then Cabral repeated the translation and everyone raised his hand.

"They'll do anything the Party asks them," said Titina. "They're the new generation."

Everyone stood up and the schoolchildren sang a very beautiful song called "Prima Linda." We met them again later that afternoon, when Cabral reviewed the two hundred FARP troops stationed at Morès. The troops were lined up in four rows and armed with submachine guns. In front of them lay three medium gauge artillery pieces, ten heavy machine guns, and six bazookas. The weapons had come from various sources: Cabral, for instance, was carrying an American rifle that had been captured from the Portuguese. A dozen cadres were standing to one side. They all wore similar uniforms and had no military rank. Cabral made a speech very similar to the one he had made to the troops at Maké. Then he turned to the children and told them to shout "On to Olosato!" (a small town then under Portuguese control). The children shouted "On to Olosato!" and walked toward the soldiers, repeating "On to Olosato!" The fighters took up the cry, "On to Olosato! On to Olosato!"

After nightfall, we could hear artillery shots punctuated by machine gun fire. Since our arrival, nightly attacks had been taking place against Portuguese posts and garrisons. The FARP would harass the posts and the next day Portuguese airplanes would try to retaliate by blindly dumping their bombs over the forest zones.

Anselmo, twenty-three years old, had completed his formal schooling at the Bissau secondary school and was the Party's man in charge of educational problems in the north. One morning we went with him on an inspection tour of the school attached to the central base camp.

"We have some forty schools in the northern region," he began. "We opened them about a year and a half ago. There are roughly one hundred pupils, age seven to fourteen, in each school. They learn how to read, write, and do figures; the teachers are members of the armed forces, and classes meet at least five hours every day. The schools are generally located in an important village, and schoolchildren come in daily from the neighboring hamlets. We explain the purpose of the school to the village people and they agree to build the school themselves, as well as benches, tables, etc. The Party furnishes the rest—things like books, writing tablets, pencils, a blackboard, and so forth. The children bring their own lunches from home. Here at the central base, we have departed from the usual arrangement and are boarding some 130 pupils, boys and girls. We have a primer made up by the Party and as soon as pupils know how to read and write there is a placement examination. For the time being we have plenty of teachers.[9]

---

[9] In its communiqué dated October 11, 1966, the PAIGC described its second teacher-training project, whose sessions had run from July through September 25: "Two hundred teacher-members of the armed forces of the liberated regions attended lectures designed to remedy inadequacies in their schooling and thereby raise the level of public instruction. Lectures on teaching methods, Portuguese, mathematics, geography, history, public health, and preventive medicine were given by Party specialists. One hundred and sixty teachers were 'graduated' when the program was over."

"Creole is the language used in first-year classes. Later on, since there is no system of spelling for Creole—it is only a spoken language—the transition is made to Portuguese. But not all of our pupils can even speak Creole when they come to us. Some have to learn it first, which comes pretty quick at their age. So it is not only a question of teaching them but of dealing with a language problem, trying to help the child make a successful transition from Creole to Portuguese—which is not so hard—or from a local language to Creole and then to Portuguese—which is not so simple. Would it have been better to create spelling systems for the local languages and then teach the people to read and write in them? We mulled this question over and then decided it would be preferable to make Creole the spoken *lingua franca*, as it were, and Portuguese the written administrative language. Since Creole is actually an Africanized version of Portuguese, several different forms are spoken: the Creole spoken by our people who live in the towns is very Portuguese, for example, whereas the dialect spoken out in the country is profoundly Africanized—deep Creole, you might call it.

"To get back to the problem of education, it must also be said that some villages have no great comprehension of the meaning or the practical use of education. The Party has to explain it again and again. We try to explain in simple terms, with pictures and concrete examples, that we are going to need a great many educated people after we expel the Portuguese. The example of those villages that have schools breaks down the reluctance of hitherto unwilling villages. And when they see results, the parents themselves push the children and make them attend school regularly. Our schools are set up for children of both sexes. The Animists have no objection to sending their daughters to school, but Islamized tribes such as the Fulahs and the Mandingos are hard to persuade. And with the girls, the custom of involuntary marriage creates a special problem we have to handle with particular care. As a result of our political lectures, the girls are no longer willing to be married off to somebody they were promised to at birth. In this very camp, for example, we have several little nurses who are no longer willing to return to their native villages but insist on staying here at the base and working for the Party. This is especially true among those coming from an Islamized background. They are considered nubile at twelve or thirteen, whereas Animist girls are marriageable at eighteen or thereabouts. The Party upholds the principle of freedom of choice. And so the parents are obliged to return the gifts they had received in advance."

Smiling, he added, "You might call it a cultural revolution—it really is."

So as not to interrupt the class, we asked the teachers—there were two of them—to go on lecturing. About a hundred boys were seated in two rows at a dozen long tables made of branches lashed together. A row of six more tables perpendicular to these was occupied by thirty girls. At front center, a blackboard was fastened to a tree. The children, who averaged between ten and twelve years old, sat on log benches, their books and writing tablets spread before them. It was very hot despite the shade provided by the trees. Occasional mortar fire was just audible in the distance. Because of wide differences of age and level, the actual teaching was being done in small groups. One group crowded around its teacher at the blackboard and took turns at exercises in long division with numbers of up to four digits. Ten or so small boys followed a reading lesson given them by an older child. Then each in turn read off a brief passage of the text from his copy of the primer. The girls were taking dictation under the direction of a teenage boy. The most advanced pupils were writing a composition, while the second teacher was giving a geography lesson to the littlest ones. The groups were all quiet and industrious. We were shown examination papers written by pupils at the end of their first year. The following is an example selected at random:

Brahima Djassi: twelve years old, eighteen months of schooling. Spoke only Mandingo. Now speaks Creole and writes Portuguese. His examination paper, two double pages long, gives some indication of the ground covered during the second school year.

1) An eight-line dictation: no errors.
2) An eighteen-line composition.
3) Arithmetic: problems of subtraction with six digits; multiplication of six-digit by three-digit numbers; a six-digit number divided by another six-digit number.

4) Grammar: Portuguese verb conjugations.
5) Problems: A man buys a shirt for 120 escudos; he then sells it for 95.50 escudos: how much does he lose on the transaction?

   I was born in 1941: how old am I? Sékou Touré is forty-seven years old: in what year was he born?

Djassi did quite well on all the questions, and the teacher gave him a grade of 16 (equivalent to a score of 80 in the U.S.).

At this point we noticed the distant hum of airplanes. It rose in a sudden crescendo as they approached. One could hear children's voices crying *"Tugas! Tugas!"* ("Portuguese" in Creole). In another instant the planes were visible. An order was given to put away the books and tablets. But the planes were already upon us. The first bomb exploded with a very loud noise, and some of the little girls screamed in terror, tore off their brightly colored blouses and threw themselves on the ground, shaking all over. As the bombs began falling around us with a terrific din, guerrilla soldiers came on the run and dispersed the children in little groups. Given the altitude at which the planes were flying, our rifles were of about as much use as slingshots, and in any case it was out of the question to give away our position by opening fire; we even turned our watches around on our wrists to eliminate glare. This time around, it was five airplanes. The crash of their bombs contrasted with the deep silence of the forest where all was motionless. For half an hour the planes wheeled over our heads with mechanical regularity. Then, at noon, they departed.

"That's it," said Anselmo. "They'll go back and say 'Mission accomplished.' They dumped all their bombs."

Shortly afterward, we learned that shell fragments had been picked up on the ground less than a hundred yards from the school. It is under such conditions that the PAIGC has, according to its own estimates, managed in eighteen months to teach 4,000 children of the northern region how to read. Four thousand is twice as many as the Portuguese sent to school in the entire country during peacetime.

Very early next morning Cabral, Chico, Oswaldo, and a number of cadres set out for a Mandingo village three hours away.

We left to join them. For a few kilometers our route lay along the Bissora-Olosato road, which since 1963 had been cut in numerous places by the guerrillas. Big trees had been felled across it. During that period the guerrillas had had nothing but pistols, and they made ambush after ambush in order to get Portuguese weapons. The Portuguese have never since regained control of the road. Roughly ten kilometers from Morès we passed an immense clearing pockmarked with bomb craters and riddled with heavy automatic fire: the former site of the central base camp of the northern region, finally spotted by the Portuguese air force but evacuated before its destruction. A few kilometers further on we passed sentinels posted by the FARP. At a turn in the path, we suddenly came out into a clearing where a large crowd of peasants had gathered. At the sight of a white man there was a brief flurry of alarm among the women that was quickly brought under control by the soldiers. In the midst of the crowd, surrounded by Chico, Oswaldo, and Titina, stood Amilcar Cabral. He called for silence, showed his rifle, and said, "We are the ones who have the guns nowadays—nobody needs to be afraid. Not all whites are enemies. Whites who are on our side are our friends. The people who are afraid these days are the Portuguese, and they are afraid because we have the guns. And the guns we have are to serve our people."

The meeting, which had been going on for several hours, was about a village (actually a group of three Mandingo hamlets) where there had been "problems." Some 250 to 300 local people were there, the men on one side, the women and children on the other. The women, dressed in indigo robes, were seated; the men, standing, wore *boubous*, or loincloths, and short-sleeved shirts of the kind sold in Gambia. It was very hot and every face was streaming with sweat.

Amilcar resumed:

"As I was saying to you, we have got to open still more schools. But the schools are worth nothing if they change nothing. Why should a little girl go to school if afterward she must be married by force? I'm telling you that the Party is not going to tolerate any more of these transactions and business deals involving daughters. Soon we intend to remove the children from the base camp and place them back in their home villages. But they are not to be married off against their will. Some of the girls came to us at the base, as you well know, in order to avoid being married against their will. A woman should marry the man she has chosen and not one her parents have chosen for her.

"The women here have been doing what they could in production and they deserve our respect for that. Meanwhile, a good many of the men have been content to go on trafficking. There are some who prefer trading in Gambia, others take their business to Casamance.[10] They buy and they sell, they sell and they buy, and finally they buy themselves a woman in order to put her to work. Now all that has got to stop. The land is good, there is no lack of rain. You have just got to get down to work. Every single man has got to work: the building of our country is not going to come from heaven. Everybody has got to work. The war is no excuse. The Balantes and Mandjaks are working, too. Our enemies are those who do not work. Here in your part of the country production has not been high enough. The Balantes are producing more and thus helping our struggle more. Here you must do as they are doing in the south of the country, where rice production has been so high that there is more than enough to go around. We can praise a person who works, but the work somebody did yesterday is not about to give him special privileges today. You have got to work every day. You have to work and keep on working. When I come back here, there has got to be rice and a lot of it. The only people who work around here are the women, and that has got to stop. They will help you and that's all. The only person who's got the right to complain that he doesn't have something is somebody who has worked and tried to get it. The Party provides guns, it provides nurses, doctors, and teachers, but it expects you to provide work. Now that we have liberated regions we don't have to ask the Portuguese for a work permit, we don't have to pay them taxes anymore, there is no forced labor.

"Some people have come to see me and when they got home have been going around with a swelled head saying they'd been to see me. However, I am no better than anybody else. The only

[10] A market town in Senegal near the "Portuguese" Guinea border. (Translators' note.)

superiority around here is the superiority of work. But there are a lot of people who like to have chiefs and the customs that go with them. In a village when two or three people are elected to be responsible, the others get mad because they all want to be chiefs. But the Party is not a system of chieftainship, the Party is here to serve the people. A person with Party responsibility is not superior to anybody, and if he does a bad job he gets replaced. What is the Party in the last analysis? The Party is the people. If a person with Party responsibility does something wrong, it is up to you to say so and get him replaced. For us the people's opinion in these matters is extremely important, because the Party is fighting for the people.

"If certain people raise their hands against you and strike you in my name or in the Party's name, don't believe them. Tell your political commissar Chico and get them replaced. You have also got to get rid of this mania of everybody wanting to be a chief. The responsible Party person gives directions and that's all. He's not there to force anybody to do anything. Also, in every village you must have a people's militia. Don't be afraid of guns. Guns are there for our people to use against the Portuguese. And if some people work for the Portuguese, it is up to you to prevent them from doing any harm. If anybody is in favor of the Portuguese, he'd better go over to their side. Those who are on our side will have the country tomorrow and have no reason to be afraid of anybody.

"What I am asking is that you should work within the framework of what the Party needs. I am asking for higher production so that our fighters can be fed, and I am asking you to accomplish things on your own initiative because everybody must participate in the struggle. From now on we will have only soldiers in the base camps. The schools and the schoolchildren will be integrated with the villages. As for the soldiers, their job will be to attack the Portuguese every day. But the soldiers must never abuse the people. We must go on being united. Soldiers who turn their guns against the people are worse than the Portuguese. I have just returned from the region of Boe. We have had victories there. We have also had victories in São Domingos. Nothing can prevent us from winning now, but the people have got to help us as much as possible and keep us informed if we are going to finish this war really fast.

"There was a time when we said, 'We are about to start the armed struggle,' and some people did not believe us because we had no guns. Now we have liberated the whole of the Oïo region as well as half the country. We told the Portuguese government a long time ago that we were going to arm ourselves and the Portuguese just laughed. They don't feel so much like laughing anymore. That's the difference between yesterday and today. We are going to win, but if you produce more, you will hasten our victory. You must work, work, work, and never collaborate with the Portuguese, neither by having business dealings with them nor in any other way. As for the people on the Portuguese side, the Portuguese are going to drop them in the end. There are already some Portuguese who know they're finished here in Guinea, but they stay on only because of Angola and Mozambique. If every person has courage we are bound to win soon.

"And what about after our victory? What will happen afterward? We are not going to have people who steal others' labor then. Because it is not only whites who steal others' labor; blacks do it, too. But we won't have any more of that here. Everybody is going to work and enjoy the product of his labor. Now you've got to tell me if you really mean to get to work."

A great many hands were raised in agreement. Cabral then had three men and one woman elected for the purpose of discussing with him the concrete problems of the zone. A few peasants raised their hands and asked for seed. Two old men spoke and started to expatiate on their personal problems and on a quarrel that had arisen between them. Cabral interrupted them and asked them to come and see him afterward.

An *homem grande* got up and said, "People here need rice. Rice and clothing."

Without giving Cabral time to answer, another old man got up and said, "Our needs mean nothing. Petty questions mean nothing. Petty sacrifices mean nothing. We must unite all the sons of Guinea. When we were still unarmed, the whites came to steal our labor and we had nothing. And now we are doing nothing. Before, we produced more and fought harder. Now they leave us alone. They try to come in their cars but they get blown up on the mines. But they still have their airplanes. And what are we doing? For several months the struggle has made no progress here. We have got to have as much heart as we did before if we are going to get rid of them for good and really win this war."

"I don't know any professors that can say it better than you do," said Cabral.

A woman got up and spoke: "I have been here since the beginning of the struggle. I have worked with the understanding that this was to liberate the people, so there would be no more slaps in the face, no more humiliations. There are a lot of people who went to Senegal as refugees after the Portuguese started bombing us. I lost one of my fingers" (she held up her mutilated hand), "but I don't feel like running. I worked in a base camp and now I am working here. I want to stick with the struggle until we are free."

"It warms my heart to hear you," said Cabral. "I wish you all courage; take heart; my message is 'Work, and confidence in the Party!'"

Everyone stood up. The children rushed to shake hands with Amilcar. The women came too. We could hear voices shouting "Schools! Schools!" and there was applause on every side. We started walking slowly to another village nearby. It was intensely hot. We ate a few mangos and splashed a little cold water on our faces. Soon the old men and village Party people who wanted to see Cabral arrived and we left him and went with Chico to visit the village school.

It was set up like the outdoor classroom in Morès, with log benches and tables made of little branches woven together with fibers. The blackboard stood against a tree. There were forty pupils, twenty-five of them girls, averaging ten years of age. Half a dozen knew how to read and write without difficulty. They had started eighteen months before and had made progress. Chico sent them to the blackboard to test their scholastic level. Others, who had not attended school regularly because they came from a neighboring village, read slowly and made many mistakes. The teacher, in uniform with a revolver on his belt, quizzed them on the meaning of the words of the national anthem and gave a good political lecture at the same time. During the class we could hear the distant sound of bombers and explosions. In one of the little girls' notebooks we saw a Portuguese propaganda tract in which the guerrillas were portrayed as half-naked stragglers with a hangdog appearance. The picture was captioned: "SO GUENTE BRUTO QUE NO BIBE NA MATO"—"These are the savages that live out in the woods."

The whole row of little girls started laughing as they watched us read the tract. We held up the picture for them to see.

"What do you think of this?" we asked.

"That stuff is no good for anybody but the Portuguese," one of them answered.

Very early one morning we left with Antonio Bana and half a dozen soldiers to visit two or three Balante villages. Sometime after seven o'clock two bombers passed overhead and dropped their bombs a few kilometers away as we continued our march. About fifteen kilometers from Morès, the Portuguese were trying to rebuild a bridge in order to make the Olosato-Bissora road usable again before the start of the rainy season, because supplies had had to be flown in by helicopter for the past few months. The heavy rains were due to start in about ten days. A couple of days earlier, FARP bazookas had destroyed the part of the bridge the Portuguese had succeeded in rebuilding. The bombers were making frequent attacks in reprisal. In the course of our hike we heard numerous mortar explosions. After three hours on the road we passed through a Balante village that had been hit by bombs. The mud huts were gutted and the trees surrounding them torn up. On the mud wall of one of these huts there was a drawing traced in black lines. It depicted a squad of eight men in formation, a truck with its driver, and beneath them three or four armed guerrillas. Two airplanes were shown diving on this scene, and three corpses were represented at the bottom of the picture.

"This," said Bana, "is one of the Portuguese' favorite spots. Whether the planes are going north or south, they always save one little bomb to drop here—just in passing."

We got a distinct view of the planes when we arrived in the first village. It was empty. There was no one but a little boy keeping watch over the village pigs. We went on toward the other village.

There, too, almost all the inhabitants had left. The fear of being bombed and the distant sound of the bombs already dropped by the planes had made them leave.

We entered the village and found three women and an old man. Our arrival did not cause any surprise. Our guide, Antonio Bana, who had spent five years in the *maquis*, was well known and appreciated, especially for his sense of humor. It was a small village, its huts huddled together. The women were preparing palm-cabbage, crushing it with blows of the pestle. An old man was bringing firewood and laying it down. A few moments later, we heard the dull explosion of a bomb. The old man came up and greeted Bana, who spoke to him. The old man shook his head and started to speak:

"You see how things are now. The Portuguese are bombing us with their airplanes. They have killed people. But many of our young people have joined the guerrillas. Independence is something we are going to have; even if we don't get it our children are going to get it and the Portuguese are going to leave our country.

"In the old days, we had forced labor. You had to work on road maintenance on the Mansaba-Bissora highway, and if you didn't work fast enough they flogged you. And when they did, they really laid it on. If you had two cows and they needed both, they would take both. You paid them taxes. A tax on everything. A tax on your wife—200 escudos. A man with several wives had to pay 50 escudos more for each extra wife. Sometimes they raised the taxes. The worse things got, the heavier they made that tax."

Now there were three planes and they were bombing much closer to where we were. We all left the village to take refuge in more heavily wooded terrain. Antonio brought along a big jug full of wine and pocketfuls of palm-cabbage. We took shelter to the sound of mortar fire that was to go on for several hours. There was nothing else to do but wait for night and calm.

So Antonio Bana, Party cadre, twenty-eight years old, told me the story of his life:

"At the beginning of my life, when I was thirteen, I worked as a houseboy for a white family in Bissau. I waited on the white man's son, served at table, ran errands, etc. I was making 150 escudos a month. One day I got to thinking, thinking about my life in the future. When I get married, I thought, how am I going to live with my wife on 150 escudos a month? After thinking it over, I decided to go out and learn to drive. An African truckdriver taught me how. But to become a driver you had to pass a test, you had to know how to read and write. And the Portuguese required an I.D. card, but since my parents were not *assimilados* I had no card. So I dropped my plans to become a truckdriver and went to work as a garage mechanic for a Portuguese boss.

"The boss had an Austin truck. When he saw I was a hard worker, he said, 'I'm going to let you drive my truck.' But he did not pay me like a regular driver with a proper license. One day he called me over and said, 'The truck is yours to drive.' I took it out, but first I asked him if I could get driving papers. He said no, but he could guarantee everything would be all right because the district commandant was a friend of his.

"I made trips inland to pick up consignments of peanuts. In order to get back to Bissau, I had a real licensed driver sitting next to me who would show his card and I would pass as his assistant. But other licensed drivers found out about it and since they were out of work themselves, they filed a complaint against me. Then the district commandant issued an order that persons without a card were not permitted to drive. And so my boss told me, 'You can't drive anymore.' So then I stayed at my job in the repair shop. I was a hard worker. The whites were free to do as they pleased. I had no right to talk back. At that time, they had the upper hand. And so it was that I worked with many white men but not one of them ever laid a hand on me because I knew how to live alongside white people: work hard and don't talk back. And when one white man had no more work for me, I would change my job and go work for another white man.

"One day—I had a friend and we roomed together—another friend came to our room and started talking. He said there was a Party. I didn't know what a 'Party' was. This friend explained that it was for independence, and the Party was created to fight against the Portuguese for the liberty of the people and to have a new life. Now I had always known the Portuguese were mistreating our people. When I was very small, I believed some people grew up white and others black, and it was the white skin that made them evil.

"When this friend finished telling us about it, we asked him questions. In a confused way, we had thought the same things ourselves. But when he explained them, everything became simple. We saw each other again several times. And that's how I became a volunteer fighting against the Portuguese.

"Since that time, I have given everything to the Party. The Party can do anything it wants with me. I worked for the Party and heard people talk about Cabral and Barbosa—that was around 1959—but I didn't know them. My job was to mobilize people. I arranged little meetings in places I knew, at first with people I could really trust, and I explained that the time had come to fight for our freedom and that the PAIGC was engaged in this struggle for our people. One day Rafael Barbosa, the president, came and I got acquainted with him. He explained the meaning of the struggle to me, and through him I came to understand many things. It was around that time that we were sent, me and some others, to the countryside to mobilize the peasants.

"We would try to get in touch with the village elders, the *homem grandes*. We did that because the old people have a lot of prestige. After that, the old men would explain things to the others. The oppression of the Portuguese was so heavy that they took us seriously, even though we were so young, and they would listen to us when we talked about independence. We explained what the Party is. The Balantes were the worst oppressed. They were always on the road gangs. They understood what we were talking about faster than any of the other tribes.

"Later on, when it came time to actually mobilize the people, Cabral made us play a game. One by one, we had to pretend, in front of him, that we were going into a village to talk to the *homem grande*. Everybody else would watch. If it wasn't right, if there was something wrong about it, Cabral would make us start all over until we found exactly the right openings and the right arguments. We would start over and over again until it came out right.

"Before going into a village to meet the *homem grande* we would try to find out all about him. You had to be very careful.

So we would find out all about the old man's daily habits, his relations with the villagers, his relations with the Portuguese, etc. At first we never went into a village unless the *homem grande* was all right, or as the Mandingos say, a 'man of confidence.' If they were men of confidence, then we went.

"You have to remember that the *homem grande* is not the village chief. The village chief is always an agent of the Portuguese, appointed by the Portuguese. The *homem grande*, on the other hand, is the oldest, the wisest, the most respected man in the village. The chief has nothing but administrative authority. The *homem grande* represents moral authority. Among my people we have more confidence in the words of the *homem grande* than in anything young people say. The *homem grande* is the center of every village's social life. Sometimes he and the village chief are friendly, but it is rare that the *homem grande* tells all the secrets of the village to the chief, because the chief is an outsider. That's how the Balantes are. And then sometimes the Portuguese take advantage of the prestige of an *homem grande* and appoint him village chief, on condition that he will work for them. The district chief is an outsider, too.

"The Portuguese impose a Muslim because the Muslims have more experience of chieftainship. Generally they impose a Mandingo on the Balantes. The district chief is not popular because he enforces the laws of the Portuguese administration. But these chiefs don't care because they have no tribal bonds with the population under them. And that is why mobilization turned out to be easiest among the Balantes.

"And so, after having found out what we could about the *homem grande*, we would arrive in a village dressed in the local style. The first thing I would do was to ask for the *homem grande*. Then, after going through the ceremony of salutation, I would ask to be granted his hospitality. The Balantes are an extremely hospitable people. The *homem grande* would answer my greeting and call for a meal to be prepared because he would expect me to stay to eat with him. It was very rare that both chicken and rice would be served. If there was only rice with some palmetto sauce, I would say, 'Papa, why aren't you giving me anything but rice? The Balantes are a hospitable people.'

" 'I am poor. I don't have any chicken.'

" 'How can that be, Papa? Do you mean that you have been working ever since you were born and you never had even a single rooster?'

" 'Why are you asking me these questions, my son? Yes, I used to have cattle and sheep, but the white man took everything away with that tax.'

" 'And are you happy, Papa, with what the white man has been doing?'

" 'I'm not happy about it. But what can I do? They are powerful.'

"By this point I had had a chance to size up the old man. He had already said he didn't like what the colonialists were doing. I wasn't doing anything but asking questions; I hadn't yet said anything. But then I would push it further:

" 'Papa, tell me, if something happened to come along that would make it possible for you to have a better life tomorrow, would you go along with it?'

" 'I'd go along with it.'

" 'Well then, you've got to get yourself ready. Right now there is a Party that is fighting against the Portuguese so that we can be free and so that if you work you can keep the fruit of your labor. If you have a son or a daughter, the Party will send them to school to get an education. But this is a secret you have to keep because if the Portuguese find out you know about it, they will kill you. That doesn't mean you can't talk about it to other people, but you have to tell it only to people you really have confidence in. Take me, for example; I have confidence in you, Papa, and that's why I came here, because I knew you were against what the Portuguese are doing to us.'

"After that, I would leave the village. I'd tell him that I would like to meet with him and a few trustworthy people from the village—outside the village in some quiet spot where I could talk to them.

"At that time, the Party was putting out leaflets. Every Party group was supposed to distribute leaflets in the city. The people living in the city come from the villages and they often go back home for a visit. If one of them knew how to read, he was given the responsibility of explaining the leaflet to the people in the village. And since I would have already contacted the *homem grande* by the time the leaflet arrived with some other comrade, trust in the Party would grow. Also, it wasn't long after that that the Party started making radio broadcasts from Conakry in all the local languages. That gave people confidence and was very important. We had to make the peasants feel that the Party is strong, too, not just the Portuguese.

"The second time I came, the *homem grande* would summon the trustworthy people so they could meet me. He would say, 'Here are the people I explained everything you said to.' And he would introduce them to me, and I would say, 'Is there anything unclear in what the *homem grande* told you about our coming struggle? Ask me any questions you need to.'

"Often they would say, 'We are nothing but black men and don't even know how to make a match. The white man has guns and airplanes. How are we ever going to make him leave our country?' And I would answer, 'Our leaders created the Party and they made it in spite of all kinds of difficulties, right in Bissau. You have to trust our leaders because soon they will have guns for us and with these guns we are going to fight the Portuguese.'

"Then after that I would ask them to explain what I had said to the other peasants of the village, so that the name of the Party and its existence would be known. In that way, people started waiting and expecting something to happen. Then I would go back to town. I was in contact with Barbosa, who was sending reports to Cabral.

"A little later, I would ask that a village meeting be held. I would explain to the peasants what the Party was and why we were fighting. I said that we wanted to get rid of the forced labor, the floggings, the excessive taxes, the theft of livestock. Then there would be a discussion period. I had to find out through discussion which people would be capable of becoming Party militants and if the village agreed I would ask them to assume Party responsibility in the village. At the very beginning there was generally only one person who could take on such a role and that was almost always an *homem grande*. The *homem grandes* were accustomed to assuming responsibilities, they knew how to speak in public, and as the moral leaders of their communities, they knew what Portuguese colonialism was because they had collided with it often enough. Then we would summon the responsible people out into the bush and explain to them what they were supposed to say to the people in their villages.

"Later on, I went to Conakry to the school for Party cadres where I took a course from Amilcar Cabral. At that time there were seven of us. That was in 1961. There were Chico, Oswaldo, Nino, who is now in charge of the southern region of the country, then Domingo Ramos, Constantino, and Texeira. They had just got back from a year of military training. Cabral first gave us a short course in political matters and then explained the tasks we had to accomplish and how we were to get them done. Then he assigned the zones in which we were to undertake political agitation and activity.

"When I came back here, I felt stronger, more confident. But the action had developed to the point where we were becoming conspicuous, and it wasn't long before the enemy started cracking down. Some of the country people got scared. Others just hardened, saying things like the Portuguese had killed their fathers, or their brothers, or their sons and that 'They're out to get me, too, and I am going to fight.' For us the crackdown was an added opportunity to explain the role played by the Portuguese in our country. The harder they cracked down and showed their true ugly face, the more they confirmed the truth of what we had been saying about them. But we also had our troubles. Some of the country people started saying it was all our fault and if we would only quiet down they'd be able to pay their taxes and live in peace. Of course, Cabral had warned us not to imagine that the entire peasantry would rise up in rapture at the mention of independence. Distrust was there all the time. You had to dress like a Mandingo to go among Mandingos, like a Balante to go among Balantes. And you had to watch out for the agents of the Portuguese who were bound to run straight to them with any information they could get on you.

"Our procedure was to speak in a village and then go out into the bush to spend the night. It was the only way we had of making ourselves and the Party known. Little by little, Party sympathizers among the village people would come out into the bush bringing us meals. Later on, we were able to call out the villagers—or at least some of them—and talk with them, explain the meaning of our struggle, and ask their help. As time went on, there were some in every village who were with the Party and others who were not actually with it but still sympathized. Then there were those who were neutral if not downright suspicious. So as to prevent this kind from doing any harm, we had to manage to isolate them bit by bit, which we did—thanks to the more determined people in each village. Believe me, mobilization is a much, much harder thing than armed struggle itself.

"I used to go back to Conakry two or three times a year. We would make our reports to Cabral and he would talk them over with us, trying to find a way of moving on to a higher phase of the struggle. He would then set new objectives and we would return.

"At the beginning of 1962, we returned as a group under Oswaldo's command. Our mission was to establish ourselves solidly enough among the people to be able to launch the armed struggle. There were eight of us. Three were assigned to the Balante zone, three to the Mandingo zone, and one to the Fulah and Sarakollé zone. Each person went to the part of the country whose local languages he was most fluent in. Oswaldo was in charge of the overall operation and was authorized to reassign us to this or that tribe, according to the work we each accomplished. At that time the Portuguese were very strong, and when they felt the population getting ready to boil over, they started descending on the villages with their troops. Our first move was to settle down in the region of Cambedge, in order to study the enemy's activities. I was sent into the Balante region to observe conditions of work and organization. When I got there, I saw that the Portuguese had tortured and killed people in many villages. The peasants advised me to clear out. Oswaldo and some others who had entered the Morès region also withdrew to the Senegal frontier. At the border we tried to attract Guineans to Casamance (Senegal) in order to propagandize among them. At that time, however, Senegal had very little use for the PAIGC.

"In Senegal they had François Mendy's MLG Party,[11] which has made many attempts to harm the PAIGC. The MLG had serious support in Senegal, but it had no contact with the population inside Guinea. Certain members of the MLG held important posts in the Senegalese administration. So at that period, Senegal had nothing to do with our Party and did not wish to have anything to do with it. The MLG did its best to induce us to quit the PAIGC. They offered us money. They said the PAIGC was a party of Cape Verdeans. When they saw that bribery wouldn't get them anywhere, they made accusations against us to the Senegalese authorities in Casamance, claiming we were engaged in subversive activities against the Senegalese government. And then they told us: 'If you want to stay here, you had better quit the PAIGC, or you'll be sent back across the border.' When they saw that that wouldn't work either, they had us jailed, claiming that we had stopped other Guineans from joining the MLG. And they mounted a big propaganda campaign against us by offering rice to the Guineans in Casamance if they would quit the PAIGC. Then Cabral arrived and convinced the Senegalese authorities to let us out of jail. When we got out, Cabral told us to go back across the frontier into the interior. But before Cabral even had time to get back to Dakar, the Senegalese authorities locked us up again. Cabral had us freed once more and accompanied us back to Conakry; from there we made an undercover march all the way across so-called 'Portuguese' Guinea till we were back where we'd started, in the northern region of our country, close to the Senegal frontier.

"By this time the worst of the crackdown in the interior of the country was over. We immediately got back in touch and redoubled our agitation effort. What with the activities of the Portuguese, who were also busily propagandizing, the entire peasant population was made aware of our existence. Which of course only increased our importance. The Portuguese in fact helped us indirectly by constantly talking about the *bandoleiros*. They went to villages with which we had never had any contact and ordered

---

[11] The Movement for the Liberation of Guinea, which initially drew its support primarily from Mandjaks living in Senegal. It is now merged with FLING (Front for the National Liberation of Guinea), a puppet party having its headquarters in Dakar.

them to turn in the bandits. The Portuguese even went so far as to offer the country people liquor and tobacco, telling them: 'Pay no attention to these bandits, Sékou Touré is trying to take over the country.' In a Balante village, they would say: 'They are going to force you to accept Islam.' In a Fulah village, they would say: 'They will force you to drink alcohol.' Meanwhile we kept busy on the counter-propaganda front, making full use of the psychological errors committed by the Portuguese. After a period of preparation, we sent for all the cadres trained in agitation work. There were several dozen, and we were able to intensify our efforts correspondingly. The Portuguese had placed agents in every village, occasionally drawn from among the local population. We embarked on a series of acts of sabotage: blowing up bridges, cutting telegraph lines, etc.

"After that (toward the end of 1962) the Portuguese launched a big offensive and forced our cadres to pull back over the border. However, those who had really managed to get their village properly together and to merge with its population remained. Within a fairly short time, the Portuguese subsided. We immediately popped up again on this side of the border. And since that time we have never left. We camped in the bush and started setting up base camps at the same time. The population knew what we were doing and helped, mainly by providing food. There were some traitors, but our people in the villages put them out of the way. In any case, there weren't very many at the time. But then the Portuguese started giving big rewards for informing. So we started liquidating the informers.

"Twice I was in a village when the Portuguese surrounded it. The first time it was a Mandingo village. The Portuguese were making a house-to-house check. I was given a big Mandingo *boubou* to put on, and I strolled out of the village wearing it. The second time was in a Balante village. They were checking people's identification. I hid in an old man's house.

" 'You seen anybody come this way?' they asked him. 'Nobody been through here,' said the old man. I got into a Balante loincloth and put a load of kapok branches on my shoulder, greeted the soldiers in Balante, and got out of there. Nobody in the village had talked. Mobilization had become a reality. Agitation was at its height. Now all that remained was to start bringing in the hardware so we could get down to direct action.

"The guns started arriving through secret channels. Back then, a gun-running operation involved a nine-day march, avoiding villages and straddling the border of the two Guineas or the Senegal line. We had a rough time in those days—you had to steer clear of both the Portuguese and the Senegalese. Nowadays it's simple: we finally got transit privileges and the guns have been getting through in regular shipments.

"Oswaldo distributed the materiel and we divided it up among our groups. Armed action started in the south around the end of 1962 and the beginning of 1963. In the north it started in June of '63. At the very outset we had seven base camps. And three guns per base. It didn't amount to much but we were getting there: one *pachanga*, which is our word for a submachine-gun, plus two revolvers. There were far more men than guns. Only the real specialists in guerrilla warfare were given the firearms, and we promptly got busy ambushing Portuguese convoys (there were a lot of them in circulation at that time) in order to seize more guns.

"At this point, a certain number of the village people we had mobilized started getting scared and many of them fled. Others avoided contact with us because of the enemy's repression in the countryside. But then others helped us with food and information on Portuguese troop movements. When the score of our successful ambushes began to mount up, people who had been avoiding us recovered their confidence and helped us. The Portuguese imagined they were going to make short work of us. But we started getting regular arms shipments and every month were able to arm a larger number of militants. Lately, as you can see, the Portuguese are pretty scarce in these parts—except over our heads, of course. Oswaldo can fill you in on the overall picture of our military operations—that's his job."

When we returned to camp at nightfall, the doctors were working on two guerrilla fighters who had been wounded by mortar fire. No one had been killed or hurt in the bombing. We said goodbye all around, for this was to be our last evening in Morès.

Maké was a six-hour march away. As usual, small squads were posted along the road at two-kilometer intervals. In the course of that night, we crossed the Olosato-Bissau highway in bright moonlight. We could make out the fresh imprint of truck tires.

Next day Cabral ordered the demotion of the two squad leaders responsible for the surveillance of the road at that point.

Djagali

About nine o'clock the next morning, as we were having coffee at the Maké base, a bomber turned in the sky high overhead. An hour later, we heard its bombs as they began to fall somewhere in the distance. "That would be in the Farim region," said Oswaldo. That morning, for the first time since my arrival in the country, Oswaldo (who had the double responsibility of organizing the various night raids intended to harass the Portuguese and of making security arrangements for the secretary-general's protection) was at last free. All of us had had a long and exhausting march the day before.

Oswaldo, who at twenty-seven is military commander of the entire northern region, spoke as follows:

"At the very beginning, well before we had launched the armed struggle, we traveled all around the country mobilizing the people. The Portuguese responded quickly with repressive measures. They made motorized sweeps—columns of trucks loaded with soldiers would drive through the countryside spreading terror among the population in the hope of rooting out Party cadres. At that point our people were forced to regroup on the other side of the frontier. Later on they returned.

"When they returned they were armed, but not well armed: there were only three weapons per group. They got back in contact with the reliable people in villages where they had already worked. There were several acts of sabotage. Then the armed struggle proper got underway in the north in June 1963. Our objective was to kill Portuguese. The Portuguese were incautious enough to venture out on the roads, not realizing that we were armed. We took them by surprise. In those months we captured a great many weapons from the Portuguese.

"Soon we had five machine-pistols and twenty-five hand grenades for each group of thirty men. The Portuguese continued to come and go, still imagining that they were going to have a quick and easy job of it. As more guns and ammunition came in both from the outside and from the Portuguese, our groups expanded. I organized new units.

"Around October 1963, four months after the start of the armed struggle, the heavy bombing raids began. It was a long time before the people were willing to leave their destroyed villages. They rebuilt on the very same sites. They refused to take refuge in the forest. You have to reckon with the fact that people in this country are afraid of the forest. A considerable change has taken place since, however, and entire villages have agreed to move into the forest and place themselves under our protection. The Portuguese used to bomb the villages by day and the peasants would go back and sleep in them every night, but since the Portuguese were using fragmentation bombs and napalm the situation became untenable. Little by little, following our advice and explanations, the peasants of the entire northern zone started leaving their destroyed villages and coming to live in the immense Oïo forest. This occurred toward the end of 1963 and the beginning of 1964.

"Arms shipments from the outside really started coming in in 1964. We set up new base camps, to decentralize as much as possible. This gave us greater mobility and let us harass the enemy a bit everywhere at once. Moreover, we were obviously less vulnerable ourselves. Following the Party Congress of February 1964, we did a great deal of reorganizing on this basis and little by little the north was secured.

"The basic structural unit of our armed forces was the group of eleven men. For certain problems there were squads of five. For important ambushes we often used groups of twenty-two. In the classic eleven-man group there was invariably a political commissar.

"At the outset of the struggle, we aimed at blowing up bridges, obstructing the highways—in short, preventing the Portuguese from moving freely from place to place. Our objective was to eliminate the small, isolated Portuguese units. Subsequently, we made night raids against Portuguese garrisons in order to hurt their fighting spirit and morale. Beginning with the 1964 rainy season, the Portuguese started making fewer and fewer sorties.

"During that entire period we had a twofold objective: to eliminate physically the maximum number of Portuguese soldiers and at the same time to organize the people more and more thoroughly. Although we were still suffering from a serious shortage of arms and ammunition at that time, by the end of 1964 and the beginning of 1965 our materiel had become somewhat more abundant. At any rate, even today we have more volunteers than guns, but at least those who are armed are well armed. And it was in 1964 that we organized our national army, the FARP. We took full advantage of the rainy season, giving the Portuguese no respite from harassment and for the most part seizing the initiative on all fronts. The beginning of 1965 saw a similar amount of action. There was a slump toward the end of 1965 and the beginning of 1966, due to our own successes and the security that was achieved as a result.

"We then proceeded to modify our political structures, setting up the interregions, the regions, and the zones. There were likewise modifications on the Portuguese side. They brought in reinforcements, both Portuguese and mercenary troops. In the beginning there were 10,000 of them; now there are 25,000. We made and have abided by the decision not to commit any 'barbarous acts' in answer to Portuguese repression. It should in fact be noted that the Portuguese do respect us—mainly of course for our strength, but also for our discipline, the reality of which is brought home to them by our very refusal to indulge in 'atrocities.' For example, it is our policy to let captured Portuguese civilians go.

"Their air force is now their main weapon. Naturally from time to time they do attempt a sweep through the liberated zones. They even try search-and-destroy operations. For example, they tried four times this year to make a sweep in the zone of Iracunda. They make these sorties several hundred strong. (In the southern region they tried to pull off a big operation on December 31, 1965. It was not much of a success. There were 3,000 men involved on their side. Our comrades in the south treated them to a riotous New Year's Eve.) They make these sorties armed with automatic weapons, mortars, bazookas, and have air support as well. Their infantrymen are equipped with Mausers and hand grenades. As they come out in such large force, we quickly know that they are on their way, having been informed either by the peasants or by our own reconnaissance patrols. We pull back. We let them push ahead into unfamiliar country. Most of their infantry consists of raw recruits who are absolutely lost out here where we have been in control since 1964. At this point, we carry out a loose encirclement, using night attacks to break up the column. Thanks to our perfect knowledge of the ground, we ambush them again and again. At times a secondary ambush is laid at one end of their line so that once serious contact has been made we can take advantage of the general confusion to launch our main attack elsewhere along the line. Not one of these Portuguese operations has achieved its principal objective: namely, to force us to withdraw from a liberated zone.

"Since 1966 the basic unit of the FARP has been a mobile group of twenty-three men: one group commander, one political commissar, and twenty-one men armed with submachine guns, plus one bazooka and one heavy machine gun. Some groups also have a mortar. These autonomous groups have extreme mobility and offensive capacity.

"As of now the Portuguese occupy only towns and fortified camps in the northern interregion. That's still a lot, and we are going to nibble some of that away from them this coming year. We are still short on materiel to arm more people. We could have a great many more combat people. Recruiting is done by the village committees. Obviously, we have only volunteers, and they are almost always very young: on the average, between sixteen and twenty-five. We are very young in general, as people's armies go: none of our cadres is over thirty. Recruits get a minimum of two months' training on our bases. First they receive basic political training, then the handling and proper care of arms, and finally elementary guerrilla techniques. The rest is learned in the field and elsewhere in daily life under the supervision of the Party.

"As for the Portuguese, their morale is very low. We have had a dozen deserters since 1964 who have confirmed this. The war is not popular among the troops. Apart from a few young ones who have acquired a taste for it and from the Salazar regime's caste of fascist officers, the infantry has no morale at all. The fliers are another matter—these gentlemen are aristocrats. And they are not liked by the troops. The troops are disgusted with taking all the losses while the fliers are dropping their bombs at no great risk and from a very safe altitude. In fact, soldiers and sailors attacked the squadron barracks at Bissau once in 1964, after their planes had bombed Portuguese troops without having taken the trouble to verify the target.

"But now the rainy season's starting. It's our big season, the phase we like to call *Pincha Tugas* because this is the time of year we wear them down and worry them to death, you know. . . ."

A combat group arrived at the base camp that afternoon with one man slightly wounded. That morning the Portuguese had tried to open the Mansaba-Morès highway. They were turned back.

We had a conversation with Amilcar about his tour of inspection and the conclusions he had drawn from it about the coming rainy season. He said, in substance, that the bases as we now know them will be immediately abolished. The schoolchildren will be parcelled out in small groups to the villages and will form the core of the future village militia. Women from the bases will likewise be reintegrated into the villages, where they will play a role in the activities of the village committees. Combat personnel will be made more mobile, to sharpen their effect. Portuguese camps must be attacked two or three times a night, as they were during our visit. Rivers must be staked out by special units whose only task will be the destruction of Portuguese boats by bazooka attack. Small units will likewise be restricted to anti-aircraft defense. The atmosphere of insecurity might affect not only the Portuguese but also the fighting men of the FARP, but for nearly a year now this has not been the case. Neither the fighting men nor the villagers have ever been so much at liberty and ease, with liberated regions firmly in hand and no Portuguese presence other than that of the airplanes, aside from a few attempted sweeps that failed; with friendly relations between the troops and a population that feels that it is protected; with secure and comfortable bases, which are all the safer because the Portuguese no longer have sufficient morale to attempt any serious offensives. All this provides the impetus to enter a new phase that will evolve during the rainy season.[12]

We could hear bazooka and mortar fire from several directions at once. Oswaldo had ordered day attacks on the Portuguese camps and particularly on the engineers attempting to repair the bridge on the Olosato-Bissora highway. A moment later, two Portuguese planes passed overhead and went on to bomb some ten kilometers away.

We left the Maké base early in the afternoon to go to the village of Djagali, about two hours' march distant. There were a score of us present—all the zone's cadres, including Oswaldo, Chico, Titina, Antonio Bana, Innocencio, and Amilcar Cabral. The majority of the guerrillas and other fighting men of the base had already left for Djagali that morning. En route we were greeted by peasants offering us mangos. At the forest's edge there is a broad, flat stretch of open ground with a few trees. A hundred men in uniform, submachine guns on their hips, awaited us. A great murmur arose as we approached.

At least 3,000 village people had gathered in two groups separated by a narrow aisle. The PAIGC had called together all the villages of the zone. As we walked between the people, we could read streamers inscribed as follows: "Long Live Independence!"; "Long Live the PAIGC!"; "Long Live the FARP!"; "Unity with the PAIGC!"; "We Will Prosper with the PAIGC!" Sitting on

---

[12] Balance sheet for the rainy season, 1966: "In July," according to the communiqués of the PAIGC, "thirty-six important attacks were made against fortified camps in the northern part of the country. Eleven camps were destroyed by mortar fire, sixteen others were badly damaged. Twenty-four GMC vehicles, UNIMOG trucks, and jeeps were destroyed. New zones were liberated in the regions of S. Domingos (northwest) and Canonungo (west). Operations were launched thirty kilometers from the capital, north of the Mansoa-Nhagra River. During August, larger tracts of arable land were planted in the north. A second rural hospital was set up. The balance sheet of losses inflicted on the colonial forces from September 1 to November 28 reached 345 dead and several hundred wounded. Thirty-three important attacks were launched, in which eight garrisons, two electrical plants, nine armored vehicles, and one airplane were destroyed."

their haunches, the balafon players accompanied the cheers that rang out at the arrival of Amilcar Cabral. There was wild applause. The beat of the toms-toms pounded in our ears. Every three feet on both sides an FARP man was posted to contain the crowd. We went the whole length of the line, moving slowly amid the shouts and cheers. At the end of the line stood rank upon rank of boys and girls, some in the FARP uniforms, others dressed country-style in loincloths. Further on were the children, who rushed forward to squeeze Amilcar's hand and tug at his sleeves.

A barrel was set up in the middle of the passage we had just come through. The shouting ceased when Cabral, stripped to a small loincloth, got up on the barrel in order to speak. Antonio Bana stood next to him, acting as interpreter, translating into Mandingo and Balante what Cabral was saying in Creole. It was a hot and muggy day and Amilcar was already covered with sweat as he began his speech:

"I salute you all in the name of the Party. I salute the *homem grandes*, for we Africans respect the old. I salute the children, for they are the future of our people. Our fight is for them. We are fighting to blaze a trail for them. I salute the women, for they are the strength of our country. They are our mothers, our wives, and our daughters. Without them, our country would be nothing. I likewise salute the men, who, with the women, are the labor power of our country.

"For me today is a day for rejoicing. There are among you people I know and others I do not know but all of you are dear to me. We need courage to carry on the fight. But when we see so many of our countrymen around us, it gives us courage and our strength is increased. We are filled with such confidence from seeing you in such a multitude that nothing on earth can stop our Party. Our task does not only consist of liquidating the colonialists, but of blazing a trail for the children of our country so that they can be truly free and we no longer have to fear anyone, white or black. Our destiny is in our own hands. We will have schools and hospitals. No one will be cheated on his labor. Ours is the road to the development of this country's true potential.

"As I have already told you, today is a holiday for me, and I wish to introduce to you a brother from the MPLA, which is fighting the Portuguese in Angola, as we are here. (Applause.) In the days of the Portuguese colonialists we used to see whites all the time; we don't see so many these days. And when we do, there is no need to be afraid because there are some whites who are friends of ours. There are those who come to make motion pictures and here is the one I want to introduce to you now. (Applause.)

"Once, a long time ago, I dreamt of being here, in the midst of my people, without the fear of the Portuguese. That was twelve years ago. When I was an engineer in Bissau I used to come out into the bush, and as I traveled I saw how tired the people were of all the drudgery and forced labor. The Portuguese did as they pleased. They took the rice, the millet, the groundnuts. They took the women, did not respect the old people, and kicked the young men around. I dreamt that some day I would return to Djagali, to a Djagali that was part of a free country with free men and women. And here I am, in liberated country, and our whole country will soon be free.

"Comrades, I see written on a streamer, 'We Will Prosper with the PAIGC!' No one should have false dreams about the future. The rice must be planted, the groundnuts must be made to grow, and nobody is going to harvest them the same day. No one will prosper and be happy without doing anything. The land must be cultivated and the rice must be tended. It's not going to be eaten the same day. Some people say that even eating is a tiring chore— but the most tiring chore of all is to become free. The thing that counts in doing that is to have a source of enlightenment, and the men and women of our people have created that source of enlightenment with their own hands. What enlightenment do I mean? I mean the PAIGC. Our Party's road is the people's road. No one dare deceive our people anymore. Our people are tired of deception. We were too long deceived by the district chiefs and the Portuguese, and that is why we are fighting for independence now.

"Independence is not just a simple matter of expelling the Portuguese, of having a flag and a national anthem. The people must be secure in the knowledge that no one is going to steal their labor, that the wealth of our country is not going into somebody else's pocket. Even today, the Guinean people stand naked and are still afraid of the river, the rain, and the forest. We tell the Guinean people that by their work the river will be at their service, the forest will be tamed, and the rain will be put to good use. Our struggle aims at giving the people work that will feed and clothe them, hospitals for the sick, schools for all the children. That is the one reason our Party exists. That is the reason we armed ourselves and will expel the Portuguese.

"The people must know that the wealth of this country is theirs thanks to their labor. We also want our people to be educated, because our people must be aware of what is happening elsewhere in the world. Djagali is not the whole land of Guinea, nor is Guinea the whole world. Our people have got to learn how men in other parts of the world are also working, suffering, and struggling.

"Comrades and brothers, our Party wants all this. Our Party is ten years old and it is struggling for this. We took up arms to expel the Portuguese colonialists, build our country, and achieve all that I have mentioned here. At the very beginning of the struggle, I sent Oswaldo and Chico to explain these things and say that we were capable of fighting the Portuguese. Many a *homem grande* said to Oswaldo and Chico, 'This Cabral you're talking about is crazy.' (Laughter.) But many another believed Oswaldo and Chico, and through the struggle what seemed impossible has become a reality. Yesterday the Portuguese came out from Mansaba and attempted to reach Morès, but our comrades stopped them and they had to go back to their camps leaving their dead behind, along with a lot of materiel. You must have heard bazooka and mortar fire through the night: that was our people attacking the Portuguese camps.

"How many years is it since you have paid taxes to the Portuguese? Three years, ever since you became free men and women. The people who go and put themselves under the protection of the Portuguese and pay them taxes are no better than dogs. The people of Oïo are proud to be free. How long has it been since this region has seen such a big meeting, with so many men and women? When did the villages ever have schools like we have now? There are 4,000 children enrolled in school in the north of our country! Under the Portuguese, there were only 2,000 in the entire country. In the south, we have 5,000 pupils. What certain people thought to be an illusion has today become a reality. And we have the guns to defend our conquests.

"Comrades, there are many parts of the country where no Portuguese have been seen for months. The colonialists are shut up in their camps and don't dare come out. Our fighters harass them daily. East of Gabu, in São Domingos, in Boe, they never make a sortie. Comrades present here can testify to that.

"Soon we are going to have a school in each village, we will eliminate the Portuguese entirely, and we will work and produce daily with our heads held high. Before everyone present I wish to affirm, and Oswaldo affirms it with me: the wet season is starting, we have arms and ammunition, and men; with these we are going to fight hard this season and the Portuguese are going to be hurt badly. In a few months all of us will see whether what I am saying is the truth. Since the fighters are intensifying their action, the people must intensify their daily work. The rains are coming and will be here within ten days.

"I must say that on the whole I am satisfied with what has been accomplished here. But the Party's watchword is 'Get more done during the rainy season.' The colonialists want to prevent our progress, but despite their bombings they cannot do it. The Portuguese know that a single bomb costs more than a village to rebuild. When they bomb, they occasionally destroy a few houses but that is not about to prevent us from winning and building other more beautiful villages. The planes are also incapable of stopping us from working. If the planes come at noon, we shall have worked in the field that morning. If they come in the morning, we will work the fields that afternoon. We will never stop, we will even work at night. No one and nothing can stop a people on the march. The Portuguese are the ones who are tired and discouraged. When we started this struggle we had nothing, we did everything with our bare hands. Now we have many guns and many fighters, but our strength is in the people who support our struggle, feed us, give us information, and send their sons into our ranks.

"Ten years have passed since our Party was born. But what

would our Party be without a people following it? The strength of our Party resides in nothing more or less than the men and women of our country, its laboring masses. To defend our people, the fighting men, sons of the people, took up arms. In this struggle there is no difference between fighters and people. Moreover, the Party is going to arm the people in all the villages and the people will thus defend themselves. In this manner, the people may be sure that their labor will not be appropriated by anyone. In this manner, the people will defend our Party and the future of our people.

"Comrades, we want to be done once and for all with fear. If we want respect, if we want to raise our heads, we must follow the Party. Today we must intensify the struggle and in order to do that we must reinforce our Party. Our Party will work with the village committees, and each village must have its committee, and this committee must work and not await the arrival of the cadres but organize itself. The cadre is not automatically the person having responsibility and authority in the village, and I want the village committee to be clear on this. The village committee works in liaison with the Party's cadres, with Oswaldo and Chico, and with another cadre, Titina Silla, who is in overall charge of our public health program in the north. She saw combat in the south, gun in hand. But now she has just got back from Europe, where she became a nurse. Comrades, we are going to place women in high-ranking posts, and we want them at every level from the village committees up to the Party leadership. What for? To administer our schools and clinics, to take an equal share in production, and to go into combat against the Portuguese when necessary.

"From now on there are going to be only fighting men in the bases. The women and girls will go into the villages as nurses or teachers, or they will work in production, or in the village militias. We want the women of our country to have guns in their hands. Likewise, the schools that have been in the bases up until now will be sent into the villages. Parents may no longer refuse to send their children to school. The men or women who refuse to send their children to school are enemies of our struggle. The children are now caught up in chores, taking care of livestock, gathering firewood, carrying water, working around the cooking fires. The old men often require the children to wash and rub them down. But the children need to go to school just as the parents need the children's help. Every adult who prevents a child from attending school will be penalized. The Portuguese didn't want us to have schools, but we insist on them. I am an engineer. Perhaps there are people present here who are smarter than I am. But there are no engineers among them because there were no schools. The Party wants to give all the children of our people a fair chance. Our people's main enemy is Portuguese colonialism. But any adult preventing the education of our children is also our enemy. Comrades, young girls are going to be coming into the villages from our bases. But don't anybody think that these girls are up for sale as brides. They will get married if they wish, but there will be no forced marriages. Anyone who does that is worse than the Portuguese. These young girls are going to work in the villages, go to school, be in the militia, and the Party will exercise complete control.

"Comrades, I am going to tell you something of great importance. Within a few years, this village is going to be rebuilt and it will be much more beautiful than it was. After independence Djagali will be rebuilt with fine houses, pure running water in every house. Electric lights will be installed. The old people may live to see this before they die. Let those who are not convinced keep this in mind: these things will come true because we are going to fight for them. We are fighting to make the people's labor benefit the people with health, a full stomach, and an open and enlightened mind. After independence, everyone will have to read and write; we can't have the people tricked by the printed page as in colonial days. Everybody knows the story of the peasant who goes to see the district chief with a paper and gets a swift kick for his pains. On the paper was written, 'Teach this idiot a lesson.' (Laughter.)

"We want all our people to have their eyes open. Anybody who has really understood our Party's struggle has grasped that. Our people have taught us many things and we respect what they have taught us. Our cadres learn from the people because the people know where things are at. But our people are also going to learn a lot from the Party. We want a new life that we will win by dint of our own labor. We are going to have machines and paved highways and still other new things you don't yet know about. This is why every person must learn to read. We cadres are going to stay in the villages and not in the cities, because the strength of our people is in the villages.

"Our Party expects that during this winter season you are going to work and produce at top capacity. We are sure that this goal will be reached. The children must work to learn; the women must hold their heads high and know that our Party is also their Party. Our Party repeats to every one of you that the road we have taken is like the Farim River: it never returns to its source but flows toward the sea. Likewise the PAIGC will reach its goal, which is the true independence of our people.

"Out with the Portuguese colonialists!

"Forward with the armed struggle and production!"

There followed loud shouts and applause. The ranks were broken and people surrounded Amilcar. The women turned to Titina in her uniform, surrounded her and talked to her all at once. And then the festivities began. People formed in groups. Mandingo women, in big robes started dancing to the tom-tom. Young Balantes danced and sang. All this was happening within twenty kilometers of the nearest Portuguese camps. Cabral stood aside for a short time to confer with the village elders and cadres. One of them came forward, saying:

"The people are happy; they have seen Amilcar. Since the Party came here, the entire people is happy. We are united. The fighting men are a part of ourselves. Amilcar has given us a light that will enlighten all Guinea. If God wills it, the struggle will soon be over."

"It is most gratifying to hear you," he replied. "There is one thing I forgot to say just now. We are about to have people's stores here in the north. All necessities will be available in exchange for agricultural products."

Several *homem grandes* stepped forward and spoke briefly to express their pleasure at the occasion. One of the old men raised his hand: "Everybody here is working as Cabral requested with regard to production in the villages, but I am an old man, I am alone because my son is a fighting man and serves on a base. How can I make my field yield more if he isn't here with me? I wish he could come home."

"I will give you an answer," said Amilcar. "The Portuguese recruit their troops by force to put us down, but we as sons of this country must fight for our freedom as volunteers. We are fighting because we want our dignity. If we don't struggle, then we return to the contempt of yesterday with the insults and the slaps in the face. For an old person like you who wants to die with dignity in a free country, it should be a matter of pride that your son is fighting on our side."

"All of us are fighting," said Oswaldo. "Our parents are alone in Bissau."

The head of the village committee addressed the old man: "First, I would like to say that if you have something to bring up, you should first bring it up with the village council and Party cadres, and not go straight to the secretary-general with it. But above all, I would like to say that I disagree with your attitude. Our sons will come home when we are free. In the meantime, it is up to us to keep up production for the struggle."

Then we strolled among the groups that were still dancing. Some of the fighting men had joined the groups and were dancing, others were talking with the village people. The sun went down slowly. When our imminent departure was announced, the groups broke up and the tom-toms and balafons joined in a single strain: everyone, village people and soldiers, danced to a march rhythm as we went on our way. And far as one could see, all along a long row of trees, thousands of peasants dancing around their fighting men who also danced, following the slow gait of Cabral, surrounded by children, walking in the rhythm of the drums.

The roar of planes passing overhead tore us from our sleep. We dressed quickly and got out of there. The planes had already started their bombing and strafing runs and were beginning to zero in on us. It was 6 A.M. A dozen B-26's turned in the leaden sky as four fighter planes zoomed back and forth. They were tracing concentric circles that enclosed us in their narrowing perimeters. This time they had come in force and all hell was breaking loose; the sudden burst and roar of napalm reached us from very nearby. We hastened to leave the base perimeter. The bombing continued with great violence for at least an hour, while we pressed our pace to get as far as possible outside the Djagali zone. An informer must have gone to a Portuguese camp during the night— the Portuguese were certainly aware of Cabral's presence in the zone. After a long march we took cover in a grove (there were fifteen of us in all) and waited for things to calm down. As the bombing grew less intense, we rested, lying under the branches or sitting with our backs against the tree trunks.

"Innocencio!" said Amilcar.

"Hmm . . ."

"Innocencio, there's a war on!"

Meanwhile, Titina was making Nescafé in a small tin can. At about 7:30 a small reconnaissance plane flew over us. Fifteen minutes later a group of peasants came by with bundles of firewood on their heads. "Balantes," said Innocencio. "The Balantes have a joking way of putting it: 'This man wants to rebuild his house before the fire has been put out.'"

The planes continued to bomb sporadically.

"Formerly," said Amilcar, "the Portuguese in the north concentrated their troops in the Oïo. Our 1964 Congress decided to carry the struggle everywhere. This was done within the year. What more can they do? They can drop bombs. But we have thousands of men under arms. The Portuguese destroy whatever they can. . . . However, they no longer control the country."

A group of fighting men showed up a little later with our things. Planes went on droning overhead, at a fair distance from us, but we continued to wait. Waiting always makes time move slowly.

Innocencio sang a popular song in Creole:

GALLO BEDJO (THE OLD ROOSTER)

What's the matter, Antonio?
What are you crying for?
I used to be a spring chicken, oh,
And I'm not one any more.

I was a tough young cock when I ate
My feed out of your hand;
I'm a sad old rooster now and you make
Me scratch for it in the sand.

Two members of the fighting forces arrived around 8:30. The Portuguese had bombed the village of Djagali and the number of dead and wounded was not yet known. Titina left immediately to supervise the treatment of the wounded.

"They would have to concentrate their forces at Olosato to get here," said Amilcar, "but we have cut the highway and the bridge is destroyed."

Nevertheless, it was decided that we would not go, as we had planned to do before leaving Guinea, to the village of Yadur. This would uselessly multiply the risks. Moreover, the measures necessary to assure the personal safety of the secretary-general are paralyzing for the fighting men and tie up too many people.

A peasant passed, carrying firewood. He greeted us.

"So you aren't taking cover?" said Amilcar.

"They can't kill all of us in a single day," said the peasant. We then learned that there were seven dead and five wounded in Djagali.

It was close to noon when we got back to the Maké camp. There we found a journalist from *Jeune Afrique*, Justin Vieyra, who had just arrived with Nino, a Party leader with overall responsibility in the south. Cabral granted Vieyra a brief interview in which he declared that the aid coming in from the African states was very inadequate.

We left for the frontier that night.

Peasants along our way greeted us with friendly salutations. Further along, two sixteen-year-old boys came up and asked Amilcar for guns. "We will have more soon," said Cabral, "and you will be getting yours." We hurried along in silence. The air was hot and muggy. Our shirts began to cling to our bodies.

We stopped briefly at a spring. The water was tepid but refreshing. Two peasants arrived, recognized Cabral, and embraced him. They were Fulahs, both of them old Party militants. Still later, we ran into a couple of young boys who saluted us.

"Keep the faith," said Cabral, "we're winning now!"

"That's a fact," they replied.

At 5 P.M. we reached the left bank of the Farim. A score of fighting men were waiting for us. We climbed into a pirogue and pushed off. Suddenly we heard an engine around the bend in the river. A voice cried, "The gunboat!" There was straining at the oars. The sound approached. We made it into the canals on the other side, where we were hidden from sight by the mangroves. The gunboat went past and the sound died away.

On the other side of the river there was a broad stretch of open ground, soggy and absolutely bare. From where we were it was about three kilometers to the first row of palm trees. Even if we took it at a trot, it would take twenty minutes to cross it, what with our weapons and other gear and the muddy ground. It was still broad daylight. The risk of being spotted by a reconnaissance plane was too great. We decided to wait until dusk. Half an hour later a second canoe arrived carrying more fighting men. Soon after that a third arrived with the last group of men. Everyone sat down. We smoked Portuguese cigarettes made in Angola: Fabricas de Tabacos Ultramarina, with the brandname "A.C."

" 'Amilcar Cabrals' we call them here," said Innocencio.

Night started to fall and we set out. A breeze had come up. One group went on ahead and another followed us. We hiked along double-time in the darkness, in complete silence.

Toward nine o'clock we ran into another group of fighters. "That's Bobo; he's in charge of the Sambuya zone," said Cabral. Bobo came up and told us what had been happening.

The Portuguese had attempted a search-and-destroy operation that morning. Six helicopters had come in with fifty Portuguese, together with African auxiliaries, at some twenty kilometers from the frontier. Bobo had assembled a fighting group of thirty-six men, and had succeeded in drawing the Portuguese into a wooded sector. The ambush took place at 5 P.M. With five of their men dead and several wounded, the Portuguese withdrew. There were four wounded in Bobo's group, three of them seriously.

We ate some mangos. Men from Bobo's group took us to see the kits taken from the Portuguese bodies. I picked one up and looked at it. "That one belonged to an African mercenary," said one of the men. It was an individual ration-kit, Type E, in a dark green cover. It contained a tube of emergency food, a water filter, etc.

We set out once more. We were now going through wooded savannah, but still preceded and followed by groups of fighting men. By way of an additional precaution, Bobo had placed two groups on our flanks at a distance of a hundred yards. We moved very fast. We covered the last kilometers, which were less wooded and thus more dangerous, in record time.

It was not long before we reached the first Senegalese village. By this time it was one in the morning, and the PAIGC ambulance had just brought in the three seriously wounded men from the ambush that afternoon.

Armed Struggle in Africa

The African Experience and Context

Since the creation of the UPC (Union of Cameroon Populations) ten years ago—the first politically organized *maquis* in tropical Africa—the *maquis* experience has been enriched, even by certain defeats. But the movements or parties that have suffered these defeats have unfortunately not undertaken a very serious critique of their actions or an analysis of their deficiencies, and have therefore impeded their own development and that of other movements by not evaluating the consequences of their failures.

1) *Maquis* organized against colonial oppression:
   —Cameroons: UPC, 1957–59
   —Angola: MPLA (Popular Movement for the Liberation of Angola), since February 1961; FNLA (Angolan National Liberation Front), since March 1961
   —"Portuguese" Guinea: PAIGC, since January 1963
   —Mozambique: FRELIMO (Mozambique Liberation Front), since September 1964
2) *Maquis* organized against neo-colonial exploitation:
   —Cameroons: UPC, sporadic activity since 1960
   —Congo-Kinshasa: CNL, 1964–65
   —Nigeria: SAWABA, attempt to organize a *maquis*, 1965.[1]

---

[1] The problems posed by the national question are particularly acute in the case of the *maquis* operating in the southern Sudan, where, since 1965, Animist and Christianized blacks have been waging a struggle for autonomy against the Arab-Moslem central government of Khartoum. Whatever criticisms may be leveled at this struggle, attempting to solve the national question with geno-

The African experience

The defeat suffered by the UPC *maquis* is doubtless the most important of all. In this case, the armed struggle against colonial oppression had begun in favorable conditions, under the remarkable leadership of Ruben Um Nyobé. The UPC was founded in 1948 on the basis of a broad political alliance. By 1955 it had become radical and it took to the countryside shortly thereafter. However, Ruben Um Nyobé, who was then secretary-general, was killed by French troops in 1958, and Mayi Matip, who occupied a key position in the party's leadership, decided to end the armed struggle.

The struggle continued, however, under the leadership of Félix Moumié, although it was directed from outside the country. Contact with the *maquis* was already weakening, and this accelerated after Moumié was poisoned in Geneva—most probably by French agents. The movement's strength was further depleted when, on January 1, 1960, France formally recognized the Cameroons as independent, thus removing one of the struggle's objectives.

Poor contact with the *maquis* and the general mistrust resulting from the assassination of the two leaders combined to lend an extremely violent character both to the leadership crisis and to the ensuing power struggle within the UPC. For a time, the two vice-chairmen—Kingué Abel and Ernest Ouandié—continued to retain leadership. Then, in July 1961, Ouandié joined the *maquis* operating in the Sanaga-Maritime region. Although there have been reports of a congress held by the *maquis* in 1963, Ouandié was probably dead by then. Meanwhile, splits were developing. After an assassination attempt against President Nkrumah in September 1962, the Ghanaian authorities ordered all residents to surrender whatever weapons were in their possession. Kingué Abel and ten UPC militants who had been granted asylum in Accra were arrested after an informer had revealed that they were still keeping weapons in their homes. One month later, Woungly-

---

cidal methods is clearly unjustifiable. See the article by C. Deffarge and G. Troeller, *Nouvel Observateur*, No. 121, March 1967; and J. Oduho and W. Deng, *The Problem of the Southern Sudan* (London: Oxford University Press, 1963).

Massaga, Tchaptchet, Michel N'dho, and several others established a "Revolutionary Committee" in Accra. Kingué Abel and the UPC militants were released after spending nine months in prison, and some of them went to Conakry, where a "Leaders Committee" had been formed around Osendé Afana. A considerable number of cadres had returned to the Cameroons, claiming that it was possible to wage a legal struggle within the neo-colonial apparatus. (Among the latter was Ndjog Aloys-Marie, the UPC Leaders Committee's representative to Cairo.)

What was happening to the UPC?

Between 1960 and 1962, more than 120 cadres had been trained in Conakry, Moscow, and the German Democratic Republic. Under Kingué's leadership, not a single one of them was sent to the interior.

By 1962, the Sino-Soviet conflict had begun to crystallize the various groups. The Leaders Committee (Conakry) was pro-Chinese. The Revolutionary Committee (Accra) was pro-Soviet. The two groups clashed with each other at the conference of Afro-Asian peoples held in Moshi, Tanganyika, in February 1963. Another group, calling itself Marxist-Leninist, was created in 1965.

In September 1965, Osendé Afana, secretary-general of the UPC Leaders Committee, and Fosso François, secretary of the "revolutionary armed forces," led a detachment of men into the *maquis*. The Accra faction of the UPC lost its base of operations when Nkrumah was overthrown in early 1966. News came that Osendé Afana had been killed on March 15, 1966, by Ahidjo's troops. Information from several sources indicates that his death was brought about by an informer.

Thus, the political climate had become one in which the principal enemy was no longer Ahidjo's neo-colonial regime but rather the factions within the UPC itself. Had the Sino-Soviet conflict deepened the rifts between the various groups or had it merely supplied them with motives for fighting each other under the cover of ideological arguments?

The first point to be made here is that the real struggle was not being waged. In such circumstances, external leadership is inevitably transformed into an apparatus where verbalizing becomes the major activity and is soon followed by intra-factional struggles—

not about the concrete action that should be implemented, but about splits resulting from external problems. This inability to solve one's own problems, this incapacity to act according to one's own national reality when circumstances are favorable, is the key to the history of all the truncated, bloodless party apparatuses that destroy themselves by inventing mad fables to explain away their failures. The problem goes far beyond the specific instance of the UPC: this was the case in Accra, it is now the case in Algeria, and in the future it will be the case elsewhere.

To substitute unconditional ties to China for unconditional ties to Russia as the touchstone of proletarian internationalism is just as wrong now as it ever was.

In point of fact, the numerous organizations that have been founded in Africa during the past few years are faced with an entirely different problem. All too often, they have established themselves abroad and have decided to wait until the international situation changes of its own accord, while they ride around comfortably to international conferences and seminars and guarantee their survival as organizations by exchanging their votes for Soviet or Chinese aid.

An organization may call itself pro-Soviet or pro-Chinese, but in fact, if it has been severed for years from its own national reality, then it is no better than a lifeless appendage.[2] Such an organization is merely the court jester of one power or another and is far indeed from participating in genuine revolutionary struggle. Experience proves that when a party is strong, when it receives the support of its own masses, and when it defines its goal as the radical transformation of its own national reality, then it will not go begging for aid.

The *maquis* operating in the Congo appear essentially to have been liquidated in early 1966, and reliable information about them is difficult to obtain. The only available texts are the *Gambona*

---

[2] It would be of great value for the UPC itself to produce a detailed analysis of its actions. Such was not the case in the recent party report presented by Koné Abdoulaye ("Problems Concerning the Revolutionary Vanguard in the Cameroons and the Unity of Patriotic Forces") at the Cairo seminar of October 24–27, 1966. This is all the more regrettable when one considers that the UPC has had a number of dedicated, well-trained cadres.

Notebooks,[3] which contain the political and military instructions issued to Congolese partisans between 1964 and 1965.

These notebooks demonstrate that the training given to the Congolese cadres suffered from a reliance upon excessively mechanical explanations and from a general lack of rigor. The class analyses offered in these texts are highly abstract. In not one single instance is an attempt made to analyze the reality of Congolese societies. As B. Verhaegen correctly asserts in his introduction, for instance, "the analysis of the Congolese peasantry bears no relation whatever to reality." And the explanation of modes of production bears no relation whatever to the various African societies in the Congo. For example: "The serf had to pay his lord a tax in the form of rent. There were three kinds of rent: 1) labor-service rent; 2) rent in kind; 3) rent in money." [4]

Elsewhere, one finds many mistakes as gross as these:

"The transition from slavery to feudalism was ingeniously prepared by the bourgeoisie."

"Feudalism made its appearance thousands and thousands of years before the modern era: its decline began around the third century of the modern era. . . .

"N.B.—The Roman empire was the last of the feudal systems. This empire and the feudal system were abolished around the sixteenth and seventeenth centuries." [5]

In any event, these texts raise the problem of how to train cadres. We shall discuss this later.

In 1958, the SAWABA party of Nigeria, led by Djibo Bakary, intended to vote against a self-determination referendum, as had Guinea's PDG in a similar instance. But SAWABA's intentions were thwarted when an agency of the French police rigged the election. Shortly afterward, Djibo Bakary escaped to Mali and then to Ghana. In 1965, SAWABA commando action resulted in complete failure: it was launched from the outside, and no serious political work had been done among the population.

African revolutionary movements have suffered considerably from their inability to establish a link between the national lib-

---

[3] *Travaux du CRISP*, No. 3, November 1965, Brussels.

[4] *Gambona Notebooks*, p. 41.

[5] *Ibid.*

eration movement and the objectives of the social revolution. In almost every case, a government loyal to the former metropolis has assumed power after decolonization. Except in Ghana, the various *coups d'état* have made no fundamental changes: the new military governments are no different in nature from the civilian governments that preceded them. When a *coup d'état* occurs, it indicates the political fatigue of the group in power and occasionally reflects the discontent of the petty bourgeoisie and the urban masses. It also illustrates the extreme fragility of the state apparatuses in question and their lack of a firm social base—in many countries, a thousand armed men need only a few hours to topple a government.

Although a number of theories correctly define the countryside as the theater of revolutionary struggle in Africa and Latin America, it is conceivable that an urban insurrection could take place in certain African countries. The social base of certain governments is so weak that their liquidation might be brought about with the help of a crisis. A firm foothold in the unions would provide the mass base of a well-structured movement that could take advantage of the disorder caused by street demonstrations and carry out armed action in a number of given areas. Such an hypothesis would be chimerical elsewhere, but it is not unthinkable in certain African countries—if the task of politicization has been accomplished among the workers. The future strength of the new government would in this case depend upon its ability to neutralize the reactionary elements in the cities, to develop a solid political structure in the unions and among the youth, and to win over the peasantry.

The problems posed by a struggle against colonialism are infinitely less complex. At present, the anti-colonial struggle in Africa is divided among the Portuguese colonies that met in Rabat in 1961 to found the CONCP (Conference of Nationalist Organizations of Portuguese Colonies). This organization includes the PAIGC, the MPLA, FRELIMO, and CLSTP (São Tomé and Principe Liberation Committee).[6]

---

[6] In addition to these organizations and, indeed, in opposition to them, are Holden Roberto's FNLA in Angola and COREMO (Mozambique Revolutionary Committee) in Mozambique.

In Angola,[7] Holden Roberto's FNLA has been faltering since 1964. The MPLA began fighting in Cabinda and last year opened a second front in the south. Nonetheless, when one considers that the struggle has been continuous over a period of six years, its achievements still appear mediocre at best—largely because the political work necessary to win over the peasantry was neglected for too long a time. Consequently, attacks are all too often launched from outside bases (Zambia) that the guerrillas use as points of tactical retreat. (See, for instance, the operations that took place in the Texeira-de-Sousa region during January–March 1967.)

In Mozambique, FRELIMO—whose political leadership is known to be heterogeneous—seems to have a firm military foothold in the northern part of the country, especially in Nyassa and Cabo Delgado provinces, which share a frontierline with Tanzania. At present, FRELIMO activity is almost entirely limited to within this zone. Party bulletins report the following results after two years of struggle (September 1964—September 1966): 3,000 Portuguese soldiers killed or seriously wounded, 175 military vehicles destroyed, 16 airplanes shot down.

The situation is far worse in the racist states of southern Africa. The abortive armed struggle in South Africa began by concentrating on urban terrorism; it subsequently spread to the countryside in 1962–63, where it was led by small groups like UMKONTO (allied with the African National Congress) and POKO (allied with a rival party, the Pan-African Congress); but it has been brought to a complete standstill by the wave of repression that took place during 1963–64. In South-West Africa, which is represented by two nationalist parties—SWAPO (South-West African People's Organization) and SWANU (South-West African National Union)—the situation depends upon international or pan-African conditions. South-West Africa's extremely underpopulated territory is, in effect, under the mandate of South Africa.

The case of Rhodesia has at least served to dispel the illusion that Wilson's Labour government might eventually aid the Afri-

---

[7] For relevant information, see Robert Davezies, *Les Angolais* (Paris: Editions de Minuit); and Gérard Chaliand, "Problèmes du Nationalisme Angolais," *Les Temps Modernes*, August 1965.

can cause. Great Britain obviously never intended to risk a crisis with Rhodesia, South Africa's staunch ally. The tottering stability of the pound depends to a great extent upon South Africa. When South Africa intervened to supply Rhodesia with oil, the so-called embargo proved to be a complete farce. The boycott on Rhodesian tobacco was never really put into practice: twenty million pounds worth of tobacco were sold to South Africa, and large sales were made to West Germany, Japan, Australia, and New Zealand. Rhodesia's other products (asbestos, copper, and chromium) were sold to South Africa, West Germany, and Japan.

The most dedicated cadres in Rhodesia's nationalist parties—and, from all appearances, especially in ZAPU (Zimbabwe African People's Union)[8]—have examined Rhodesia's relative diplomatic isolation and are beginning to conclude that they alone are in a position to modify the conditions of the problem they face. The task at hand is to prepare the armed struggle by seeking support from the peasantry on the reservations. This would allow for an improvement upon the conception of Zambia-based commando sabotage raids.[9]

The African context

The movements struggling against colonialism or the racist states have received little assistance from the Organization of African Unity. The OAU was founded in 1963 amidst great enthusiasm and confusion. It announced all sorts of contradictory ambitions and soon revealed its conservative nature. At the OAU's last session in March 1967, the Committee for Aid to National Liberation Movements was harshly criticized for "incurring excessive administrative expenses and for subsidizing certain individuals who spend funds on maintaining a high standard of living for themselves, instead of allocating them to the struggle." [10] In early 1964, the entire organization had already been subjected to the same kind

---

[8] ZANU (Zimbabwe African National Union) is the other nationalist party.

[9] We shall not discuss here the case of the Spanish colonies, of Djibouti, the Comores, and Réunion.

[10] *Le Monde*, March 7, 1967.

of criticism:[11] it was spending more money on its own operating budget than on aid to struggles.

Very few states supply national liberation movements with either logistic or financial support. Nkrumah's downfall was a very hard blow for a considerable number of movements. At present, Algeria gives genuine aid to most of the movements; Tanzania aids Mozambique's FRELIMO and Rhodesia's ZANU; the Congo (Brazzaville) aids the MPLA; Guinea aids the PAIGC; and Zambia aids the MPLA and Rhodesia's ZAPU. Since Nkrumah's downfall, not one state in tropical Africa has contributed concrete aid to movements engaged in a struggle against neo-colonialism. In 1962, for instance, Mali sought to normalize its relations with Nigeria by asking SAWABA to leave its territory; then in 1964, it expelled the AIP (African Independence Party) in order to resume diplomatic relations with Senegal. During this period, several groups of armed AIP men were intercepted along the border between Senegal and Mali.

No revolutionary government in Africa has yet managed to break with the imperialist powers, to strengthen its own national independence significantly, or to lay a solid foundation for economic and social development. At the very best, a few states have largely succeeded in extricating themselves from the domination of their former colonizers by more or less nationalizing the crucial segments of their economies, by diversifying their exchanges and the sources from which they receive foreign aid, and by implementing independent foreign policies. This has, to a varied extent, been the case in what some call revolutionary Africa: Tanzania, the Congo (Brazzaville), Mali, Guinea, and, until recently, Ghana.

After making a tour of capital cities in 1963, Chou En-lai declared: "The revolutionary situation in Africa is excellent." Nothing could be further from the truth. After a few short years, the façade of socialism has collapsed and African realities have begun to appear in their true light.[12] Since 1960, when a number of countries received their formal independence, the important new phenomenon has been the significant intervention of the United States.

---

[11] *The Spark*, Accra. Reprinted in *Révolution Africaine*, No. 53, January 1964.

[12] See "L'Afrique dans l'épreuve," *Partisans*, Nos. 29–30, May–June 1966.

British and French imperialism certainly retain much of their traditional strength, but the past few years have clearly shown the concerted advance made by American interests. In the general imperialist offensive of which Vietnam represents the high point, United States pressure has been less spectacular in Africa than in Asia or Latin America. The U.S. has sought to disguise the true nature of its African intervention by importing "liberal" personnel with anti-colonialist pretensions. Future struggles will have to take this new context into account.

In 1960, U.S. economic relations in Africa were narrowly confined to Liberia, Libya, Ethiopia, Morocco, Tunisia, Ghana, and South Africa.[13] But within a few years, American trade, aid, and investments have increased considerably.

Africa sends 9 percent of her exports to the United States, as against 19 percent to Great Britain and 18 percent to France. It receives 11.5 percent of her imports from the United States, as against 17 percent from Great Britain and 18 percent from France. In 1960, American investments in Africa totalled $867,000,000. By 1964, they had increased to $1,629,000,000. But when it issued this figure, the U.S. Chamber of Commerce did not include indirect investments. According to official estimates, the latter amounted to $2,500,000,000 in 1964, when American investments represented 16 percent of all foreign investments in Africa. This figure was estimated to have risen to over 20 percent in 1966. For the most part, these investments are placed in Libyan and Algerian hydrocarbon, Liberian and Gabonese iron, Zambian copper, Gabonese manganese, Angolan diamonds, and, especially, in the various mining concerns of Rhodesia and South Africa.

The U.S. devotes 28 percent of its total foreign aid to Africa as against 58 percent to Western Europe. This aid is distributed in the form of loans, accessory aid, gifts, technical assistance, the Food for Peace program, and the Peace Corps. Considerable military aid has been sent to Ethiopia, and, more recently, to Morocco and Tunisia, among others. In 1966, for instance, military aid to Morocco increased from $2,300,000 to $4,500,000, making a total of $30,500,000.

---

[13] "The United States and African Economic Growth," *La Documentation Française*, No. 2,689.

To one degree or another, America now makes its presence felt in many African countries. First come Liberia, Ethiopia, Nigeria, Ghana, Guinea, South Africa, and Libya; next, Rhodesia, Kenya, Zambia, the Congo (Kinshasa), Morocco, Tunisia, and Sierra Leone; and finally, to a lesser degree, Gabon, the Ivory Coast, the Central African Republic, Togo, Madagascar, and Uganda.

The Objective Conditions of the Armed Struggle

A significant portion of the African continent, in terms not only of area and population but of the immense wealth of its natural resources (especially in southern Africa), still remains beneath the colonial yoke today. It is primarily in these countries that the problem of armed struggle has posed and continues to pose itself.

Armed struggle has been undertaken and waged with varying degrees of success in Angola, Guinea, and Mozambique. Although the struggle has not been initiated in South Africa and Rhodesia, objective conditions exist: in neither country is there the slightest possibility of "dialogue" with the white racists who hold political power, and the situation will not be modified by anything short of armed violence. The nationalists must count chiefly on their own strength; the aid they will receive from other African countries will be limited. Preparation for the armed struggle is the order of the day: the future will belong not to the party that has the most progressive program but to the nationalist movement that is most capable of drawing the masses into the armed struggle.

Throughout the remainder of tropical Africa, formal independence has already been achieved—within a neo-colonialist context. There is no need to repeat here the familiar analysis of neo-colonialism and of the pitfalls of foreign aid, or to refer to the establishment in these countries of administrative bourgeoisies that are mere appendages of imperialism.[14] Nevertheless, it would hardly be scientific to ignore certain objective conditions that are at pres-

---

[14] Gérard Chaliand, "Indépendance nationale et révolution," *Partisans*, Nos. 29–30, May–June 1966.

Table 5

United States Economic Relations with Africa

Country	Exports to U.S. (1964) (in percent)	Imports from U.S. (1964) (in percent)	U.S. aid (1965) ($ millions)	U.S. investments ($ millions)	Remarks
Algeria	—	7.9	17.5		Important capital investments in French and Dutch oil companies
Angola	25.8	8.7	—	18	Hydrocarbons, diamonds
Burundi	70	6	1.1		
Cameroons	7.3	4.2	5.5		
Central African Republic	15.2	5	0.7		
Chad	—	7.5	2.1		
Congo (Brazzaville)	—	5	2.4		Phosphates, bank
Congo (Kinshasa)	12.2	28.4	25.5	25 direct 50 total	Less than 2% of all foreign investment
Dahomey	1	2.3	1.1		
Ethiopia	49.4	8.6	18.8		Hydrocarbons (research & distribution), potassium
Gabon	18	12.6	1.1	80 (?)	Manganese, iron
Gambia	—	1.2	0.1		
Ghana	21	8.7	2.3	201	Loans for the Volta dam; aluminum foundry on the Volta
Guinea	1.5	30.4	21.7	75 (?)	Aluminum foundry in Fria (48.5% Olin Mathieson)
Ivory Coast	20	9.3	4.3	6 (?)	Oil refineries, banks, diamonds
Kenya	9.1	6.4	9.2	57 direct 100 total	Distribution of hydrocarbons, extensive industrial investments
Liberia	29.5	35	41.3	187 direct 275 total (?)	Rubber, iron mines, more than 50% of all foreign investments

Country	Exports %	Imports %	Aid	Investment	
Libya	4.2	23.2	1	382 direct	Hydrocarbons, one-third of all investment
Madagascar	19.6	4.5	5.3		
Malawi	3	1.8	3.2		
Mali	—	1.1	1.8		
Mauritania	3.1	17.8	—		Copper mines
Morocco	1.2	9	37.4		Commercial investments: oil products, tires, etc.
Mozambique	4.8	3.8	3		Oil drilling, 15% of all foreign investment
Niger	—	3.7	1.4		
Nigeria	6.7	11.4	33.3	150 (?)	Oil drilling, hydrocarbons, banks, textiles, government loans, & indirect participation
Rhodesia	3.3	6.8	—	56 direct / 105 total (?)	Lithium & chromium mines, oil refinery, capital investments in European mining companies
Rwanda	18	2	0.2		
Senegal	—	5.3	1.5		Distribution of hydrocarbons
Sierra Leone	1.5	4	5.6		Mines
Somalia	2.5	6	7.8	15	Distribution of hydrocarbons
South Africa	8.5	19	—	467 direct / 963 total	Gold, various ores, oil refinery, etc.
Sudan	3.2	6.9	7.6		Textiles
Tanzania	8	5.7	6.9		
Togo	10	3.1	1.4		Distribution of hydrocarbons
Tunisia	—	10.2	54.1		Distribution of hydrocarbons
Uganda	27.5	4.1	2.5		
Upper Volta	—	—	1		Harvey Aluminum in Boké, etc.
Zambia	2.7	5.2	1		Copper

Note: The percentages for exports and imports have been taken from figures given in the *Direction of Trade Annual 1960–1964* of IMF-IBRD. Figures for aid received come from the U.S. State Department. Investment figures were compiled by the U.S. Chamber of Commerce. Figures followed by a question mark are minimal estimates coming from either the U.S. administration or private sources. The above tables have been excerpted from *Le Mois en Afrique*, No. 3, 1966.

ent unfavorable to revolutionary development through armed struggle.

A *peasantry without the problem of agrarian reform*

In most of the countries of tropical Africa, especially in the west, the peasantry is not faced with the problem of agrarian reform.[15] In Africa as a whole, the proportion of wage-labor on the land is extremely low. The thirst for land that is such a mobilizing force in Latin America, Southeast Asia, and the Arab countries is largely lacking in Africa. Moreover, the African peasantry lives in a subsistence economy, which although harsh has never presented the problem of mass starvation. This is directly related to the low population density of tropical Africa, where there is only one country with a population over twenty million, and where the population density of many others is ridiculously low—in few does it exceed ten inhabitants per square kilometer.

The lower middle class, natural holder of political power

The lower middle class, whose social importance in underdeveloped countries is considerable, has in tropical Africa found a niche for itself in the numerous government bureaucracies and takes to this role with ease. It is not, as in many Latin American or Middle Eastern countries, a class excluded from posts of responsibility and leadership by landlord oligarchies and comprador bourgeoisies. It is not necessary for a portion of the lower middle class in tropical Africa to move to the left in order to come to power as a class in the neo-colonial states.[16] As the one and only class possessing knowledge, organization, and "know-how," it already has political power in its hands. (In this context, "struggle" becomes primarily the struggles among tribes and clans.) The number of persons in the opposition who at one time or another during the last half-dozen years rallied to the various regimes of the neo-colonial countries is proportionally such that the problem must now be seen in

---

[15] Notwithstanding the obvious examples of Kenya and a few other countries (Ivory Coast, Ghana, Angola, etc.) where local and foreign planters hire day-laborers on their plantations.

[16] This is what the Egyptian lower middle class had to do.

terms not of individual defections but of the social base of these opposition members.[17] In tropical Africa, social discontent remains at present essentially an urban phenomenon. It should be pointed out that almost everywhere the bureaucratic bourgeoisie is more numerous than the proletariat.

The low level of productive forces is obviously the major handicap and to a great extent explains the foregoing. Historically, this low level has several causes, of which the slave trade is not the least: from the fifteenth or sixteenth century on, this hemorrhage of productive forces prevented Africa from experiencing a normal development. And the low level of productive forces accounts for, among other things, the fact that the cleavage of classes and the antagonisms arising from them are much less sharp in tropical Africa than in Asia, Latin America, or in the Arab countries.

But these antagonisms are developing rapidly, primarily through the establishment and strengthening of a corrupt administrative bourgeoisie. The lumpenproletariat created by the exodus from the land is swelling rapidly. The relatively well-developed educational system is about to throw on the market trained people who will not be able to find jobs, while little by little the peasantry will see its needs grow and yet be unable to satisfy them.

It is nonetheless doubtful that in the near future guerrilla *focos* can be established and can play a role of any importance in countries where independence has already been reached on a class basis. Relatively favorable conditions exist in Nigeria although they have already been largely ruined by tribalism, but social contradictions that produced them transcend the context of regional antagonisms.

In most of these countries, the problems of tribalism have not been treated with sufficient seriousness and understanding. Ruling groups, who in many cases were politically educated outside their

---

[17] In Morocco, for example, the lower middle class is discontented to the extent that the regime does not offer it the possibilities of rising to the posts and functions of responsibility and power to which it aspires; it has not been integrated with the ruling class. A revolutionary situation exists in Morocco, but remains unexploited by the reformist leadership of the UNFP. There is a landless peasantry, massive migration from country to city, chronic urban unemployment, an extremely small ruling class. The entire society is in crisis and owes its stability only to a military and police regime in the cities, the absence of revolutionary agitation in the countryside, and repeated injections of dollars.

own countries, have had a tendency to apply class criteria mechanically, without taking account of the tribal realities. This is an essential problem and requires a special analysis adapted to actual local conditions.

In the African context, the low level of productive forces makes it necessary that political work directed toward breaking down magico-religious superstructures be carried out with the greatest tact and delicacy.[18] If this job is well done, the people's war of liberation can by its very development reduce the hold of magico-religious beliefs. On the other hand, if sufficient attention is not paid to these beliefs, they may become a considerable hindrance to the organization of the struggle.

Political Strategy of Guerrilla Warfare

There is no point in theorizing on the basis of a single experience and making of it a model having continent-wide, if not worldwide,

[18] ". . . the Portuguese ground forces were unable to get back; the air force was sent instead. The people were not clear on what was happening; they had the idea that Mbuta Muntu was coming to give us our orders and, when they saw an airplane, thought it was him, so they congregated and started praying: Mbuta Muntu has come, let us pray, he has come to give us the word. The Portuguese took advantage of the people being congregated like that and started dropping bombs, and so after many were killed, the people found out that it wasn't Mbuta Muntu, it was the Portuguese Air Force."—Robert Davezies, *The Angolans* (Paris: Editions de Minuit), p. 33, "Ciel."

"But one kilometer outside Ucua four trucks and a jeep came up behind us on the road. Mbuta Muntu's orders were not to look backward. The commander prayed. Then he ordered us to about face and look at the enemy. The Portuguese were already firing on us. The commander picked up a stone, threw it at the Portuguese trucks and shouted 'UPA!' We rushed the trucks."—*Ibid.*, p. 67, "Gabriel."

"We killed thirty white men, we killed the post commander of Ucua, and we killed a big white witch-doctor, José Matias. He was the proprietor of the Hotel d'Ucua. He had been firing at us from a second-story window. He had a naked woman in the room with him, it was his wife, and a kettle with a snake in it. Before shooting he put his bullets into the kettle and then inside the woman's body for a moment, then he fired. Unhappily for him one of these bullets fell out the window, cartridge and all, unfired. The nationalists got it. They shot at him and it was this bullet that killed him. We found him dead, squashed on all fours against the ceiling."—*Ibid.*, p. 65, "Gabriel."

validity; this would amount to underestimating specific conditions in individual countries. Nevertheless, some features revealed by an analysis of the struggle in Guinea seem to be a valid basis for a certain number of generalizations.

First of all, contrary to the theory of the *foco*, and above all contrary to the mechanical application of this theory[19] in a number of Latin American countries (Peru, 1964; Ecuador, 1962; Colombia, 1961; Paraguay, 1962; Argentina, 1964),[20] the PAIGC got underway only after a protracted phase of preparatory political work undertaken in view of special conditions obtaining in Guinea. Why?

It is not enough to say that support must come from the poor peasantry and the proletariat. It is still necessary to find out which are the most sensitized and easily mobilized sectors of the population, those having the strongest subjective and objective motivation to revolt. Experience has shown that it is not enough to assimilate the gist of revolutionary theory: beyond this, it is absolutely necessary to be able to determine the specific characteristics of the national realities in question. This is not the case in the leadership of many a revolutionary movement, inside and outside Africa.

Nor is it by any means an evident truth that the poor peasantry is spontaneously receptive or rapidly drawn to joining the ranks of the revolutionaries. There are blocks that retard the process. It is absolutely necessary in any given situation to find out what they are and what causes them, *before* having to overcome them.

Obviously, it is not a question of disputing the principle of armed struggle, which in many countries is the only possible way to change the existing social order. It is rather a matter of refining the technique of implantation as much as possible, of giving the struggle strong roots, which is the first phase of guerrilla war. Be-

---

[19] See A. Pumaruna, "Révolution, insurrection, guérrillas au Pérou," *Partisans*, No. 31. [This article was published in the U.S. in *Treason*, I, No. 1 (July 1967).—Trans.]

[20] Régis Debray, "Le Castrisme: longue marche de l'Amérique Latine," *Les Temps Modernes*, January 1965. On the *foco* theory, see R. Debray, *Revolution in the Revolution?* (New York: Monthly Review Press, 1967). See also Henry Edmé, "Révolution en Amérique latine?," *Les Temps Modernes*, May 1966.

sides, at bottom the debate is not so much one of the pros and cons of implantation, but rather—the need for this being granted —of the most effective means of achieving it. The theory of the *foco* as systematized by the Cubans for the Latin American context has, among other merits, the advantage of bringing out into the open the political sclerosis of the many Latin American Communist parties that are bogged down in legalism, electoralism— in a word, in reformism. This type of legalistic coexistence always turns out to benefit those who possess the instruments of power. The action of the Party, on the other hand—and sometimes its very survival—continue to depend on police and military repression or *coup d'états*.

Thus in Guinea armed struggle had been prepared for long before it began. This preparation consisted of reconnaissance in the field, together with political agitation and propaganda work. It is through this process that the PAIGC, forged between 1956 and 1959, tempered its steel between 1960 and 1962.

The usefulness of this political work in mobilizing the peasantry should not be overestimated. It is only the groundwork; it does not of itself win over the peasantry. From this standpoint, political preparation amounts to psychological mobilization, nothing more. It would be an error to think the contrary.[21]

---

[21] "In 1935 an army calling itself the Red Army arrived. It was in the countryside. The K.M.T. [Kuomintang] was in the towns. This Red Army made propaganda and told us: 'The Red Army is good and we are going to divide up all the land and you won't have to pay taxes or rent to anyone any longer.' It was in the month of February 1935 that I met communists for the first time. . . . They came to us one night and told us: 'We are propaganda-makers for the Red Army and now you are to make a revolution.' We replied: 'All right, we will.' But we didn't think they had any real power; they did not look as though they had and what could we poor farmers do? So we did nothing.

"But in March of that same year, they came back again. They called us all together for a meeting outdoors and told us to form a poor farmers' association and elect a leader. . . .

". . . To begin with, people were afraid of them and said that communists were murderers, but when they came here they were ordinary people and they always said: 'Divide up the land and fight against landowners and despots.' They talked a lot and held lots of meetings, and at the meetings we used to stand up and shout 'Yes, yes!', but we did not not really believe in them or that they had any real power."—Jan Myrdal, *Report from a Chinese Village* (New York: Pantheon Books, 1964), pp. 66–67.

However, without this preparation (and it can be made under arms) any guerrilla action runs the risk of being transformed into an isolated commando strike, whether launched from the other side of a frontier or from bases hidden in the mountains or in the forest. In either case the guerrillas are cut off from the people, whom they must avoid almost as carefully as the enemy; lacking political control of the villages, they have to beware of the agents the enemy has not failed to plant there. This, for example, is what has happened in Angola.

But the prime goal of this reconnoitering phase is to determine with precision which sectors, levels, etc., of this differentiated peasantry are the most conscious of existing oppression and there-fore readily receptive to being mobilized against it. In other words, it is a matter of finding the tinder to strike the spark. This ques-tion requires the most meticulous attention and necessitates a real knowledge of specific local conditions. More often than not this is precisely what has been lacking.[22]

In "Portuguese" Guinea, historical conditions have made the Animists the most easily mobilized part of the population. While

---

[22] A fact which the Organization of Latin American Solidarity (OLAS) has recognized:

"A sociological investigation of anti-imperialist character is now underway in twenty-nine Latin American countries. It is being carried out by the na-tional committees taking part in the first conference of the Organization of Latin American Solidarity (OLAS).

"The questionnaire, covering six important topics, has been sent to progres-sive public figures, historians, sociologists, and others engaged in scholarly re-search, as well as to progressive organizations throughout Latin America. Several thousand persons in Cuba are presently engaged in this investigation, in which various organizations and institutions of the Revolutionary Govern-ment are participating under the guidance of the Communist Party.

"The objective of this OLAS project is to determine the actual situation in all countries involved as well as the degree and the forms of enemy penetration into Latin American society as a whole."—*Prensa Latina*, Bulletin No. 916, March 5, 1967.

A similar project was undertaken two years ago by the United States, with of course opposite ends in mind. The idea was, using investigations that can be characterized as "sociological espionage" (Project Camelot in Chile, Simpático in Colombia, etc.), to identify the discontented sectors and classes of the population and thus learn where to direct the greatest efforts to head off trouble.

engaged in the "pacification" of the country at the turn of the present century, the Portuguese depended heavily on the Fulahs and reinforced Muslim–Animist antagonisms by imposing Muslim chiefs on the Animists. They thereby succeeded in making the Muslim chiefs as a whole, and especially the Fulahs, a valuable auxiliary. The institution of chiefs naturally has deep roots, and it is not simple to tear away those who live under it.

Winning over a minority in order to make it an instrument of indirect domination is a classic historical phenomenon. On the other hand, the Portuguese invaders encountered stubborn resistance from the peoples of the Oïo forest, the Balantes, the Balantes-Manés—apparently less affected by colonialism—as well as the Pepels, who had formerly dealt in slaves with the Portuguese on a basis of strict equality, before they too were subjugated: all these were quickly mobilized for the armed struggle. It is first and foremost on these layers of the population, uninhibited by chiefs loyal to the Portuguese, that the PAIGC was able to depend, while at the same time steering clear of tribal problems and going on without hesitation to win over the Mandjaks and the Mandingos and making a special effort to solve the Fulah problem.

At the same time, the PAIGC strove to unite the Cape Verdeans and the Guineans against Portuguese colonialism. The Cape Verdeans,[23] not being classified as "natives," have often served as auxiliaries in the administration of other Portuguese colonies and have to a certain extent been instruments of indirect domination. But they also constitute (at least a large proportion of them) the stratum most conscious of colonial subjugation. And so the PAIGC has worked very hard to overcome any substantial divisions among these atomized groups that compose every colonialized society.

Naturally, there exists no single example of a national liberation struggle which has created absolute unanimity among the people. Even after seven years of war, the Algerian *harkis* still continued to fight against the FLN. Similarly, African mercenaries are found fighting on the Portuguese side. They do not form a distinct unit —there is no unity among African mercenaries—but are appor-

---

[23] On this problem, see Dulce Almada, *Les îles du Cap Vert*, PAIGC, 1962; and Gérard Chaliand, *Guinée et Cap Vert en lutte pour leur indépendance*, cited earlier.

tioned out in little groups in the colonial units as guides, interpreters, and soldiers. According to Portuguese deserters, their percentage is rather low.

The phase of primary mobilization enabled the PAIGC to determine, on the spot, where to concentrate its first efforts. In Africa the intellectuals who form the leadership core of a party all too often have little interest in the countryside—not that they fail to recognize its importance on paper; they simply do not have the taste for it personally and in fact feel definitively estranged from it. Too many parties in exile use up financial aid without being effective in the field, primarily because they are never to be found in the field. How are they to mobilize the peasants from whom they are so separated? And the struggle waged from a foreign exile offers them other advantages: far from being a renunciation, it is a means of social and financial advancement.[24]

Paralleling the problem of the psychological mobilization of the peasantry and of determining the sensitized sectors of the population, there is the problem of forming middle-rank cadres. Their number has generally been insufficient.

What is needed are cadres of middle rank from among the people, cadres who, once politically armed, can speak to the peasants in their own language, using arguments that move them and are a reflection of their day-to-day problems. The lack of such cadres is the tragedy of the great majority of abortive *focos* in Latin America.

Higher-rank cadres generally, if not always, come from the lower middle class. Since the principal field of the struggle is the countryside, it is a good idea to have the middle-rank cadres come from there. It should be mentioned in this connection that it is important that the political education of these cadres be directly linked with their local reality and not be based on schematic textbook generalizations. For the most part, cadres sent to socialist countries for training—no matter to which one—receive a general the-

---

[24] Here again we have the problem of the discipline and style of the party. And here again homage is due the PAIGC. Its foreign representatives have almost always been sober and hardworking militants who were seriously doing their job on a shoestring budget in such a way as to win the PAIGC the respect of militants in the countries where they have been assigned.

oretical education that needs thorough rethinking in the light of the realities at home before it can be put to use. It is up to the leadership to articulate theory in the light of practice. This is precisely what the PAIGC has been able to do, while at the same time itself training the maximum number of cadres. The training school for cadres organized by Amilcar Cabral at Conakry has been a prolific source of middle-rank cadres.[25] Mobilized by the agitation work being done in the countryside by already trained cadres, young people come for a political education adapted to their concrete problems, and having received it, go back into the *maquis* to carry on the job of agitation and mobilization.

The three features of the struggle we have just discussed are part of a single process and arise from the initial phase of guerrilla war —the phase of implantation, in which a liberation movement takes root among the people. This phase is difficult. The peasants, crushed by taxes and exploited though they may be, are still not in the position of having only their chains to lose. Repression, airstrikes, punitive expeditions ("sweeps," etc.) are bound to hurt them first. Obviously, the peasantry is going to be won over only by concrete achievements, such as abolition of the colonial tax and forced labor, or an agrarian reform carried out to meet local needs. But these acts by themselves are not decisive unless they are accompanied by tangible proof of the guerrillas' ability to fight against the colonial army and win. It is necessary to create an entirely new and favorable military situation if the peasants are to be drawn into genuine participation. Unless the guerrillas are capable of creating the conditions for the local defeat of the enemy, and, at least initially, of furnishing the peasants some degree of protection, the rebels will not have a following. The guerrillas must, in short, supply tangible proof that they are at least as powerful as the colonial army.

And so the phase of military implantation—once the preparatory political work has been completed—must be particularly dynamic: it should in fact be achieved in a lightning stroke. Which naturally implies that while the political groundwork is being laid, spe-

---

[25] A certain number of cadres have also been trained at the Université Ouvrière in Conakry.

cialized guerrilla commandos have been organized and trained. This, too, was done by the PAIGC.

The second phase of guerrilla war, that of its development, implies a considerable effort from the political standpoint alone. Gradually controlling greater and greater areas, more and more people, a liberation movement is faced with the necessity of doing a regular job of political indoctrination among the peasantry, so as to draw it fully into the struggle and raise the general level of political awareness. The best method seems to be to give maximum encouragement to the villagers' own organization of their villages, under flexible Party control. In our opinion, this work requires political commissars. If such officers are considered useless under the *foco* theory,[26] this stems from the fact that the *foco* rebel army consists solely of cadres from the urban petty bourgeoisie. This is not the case in Africa, it was not the case in China yesterday, nor is it the case today in South Vietnam.

Experience seems to show that a great deal of attention must be focused on preventing the guerrillas—at least a certain section of them—from becoming detached from the peasantry. Is the mere fact of having started the struggle on the behalf and in the name of the masses a guarantee against losing touch with them? Tribal and patriarchal structures in Africa create a tendency to accept unquestioningly the authority of the local leader. There is thus a tremendous temptation for certain local Party chiefs to display authoritarian tendencies when they have been given too much independence and not enough Party supervision. The excessive independence allowed during the first year of the struggle in Guinea had already produced a few petty tyrants by the time the Party Congress held in the *maquis* in February 1964 was obliged to get rid of them.

Naturally, there is no such thing as a dichotomy between the party and the guerrilla army. The guerrilla army is the party in arms. But care must be taken to maintain the closest possible symbiosis between army and people. There must be continuous

---

[26] See *Revolution in the Revolution?*. Similarly, according to the *foco* theory "the rebel army is the nucleus of the future party"—which is highly improbable. The party, on the other hand, is very well able to form the core of the guerrilla army. It all depends, finally, on the nature of the party.

interaction between leadership, cadres, guerrillas, and peasants through information, explanation, dialogue, and the exchange of criticism.

It is up to the leadership to insure the proper working of this process. There is no need to emphasize the fundamental importance of a unified leadership. Crisis at the top level of leadership is the beginning of a movement's decomposition. There is no point in agonizing over the role of the individual in history. An uncontested leader remains at the present time the safest way to insure the homogeneity of a party's leadership. This advantage is, to be sure, balanced by the difficulty of replacing him and by the fact that too often the solution both of complex and everyday problems is expected of him alone.

Despite the war and the discipline it implies, the right to criticism is the surest source of democracy: moreover, it permits the rapid correction of errors. Errors should be recognized and not hidden under the pretext that acknowledging them would help the enemy. What really helps the enemy is not so much the recognition of errors but the errors themselves. On a movement-wide scale, the fact of systematically masking errors, the refusal to let reality be known, ends in a "bluff" disguised as psychological warfare. But whereas psychological warfare *accompanies* warfare, this kind of bluff becomes a substitute for warfare. A proof of the strength of the PAIGC can be seen in its willingness to display, through this book, its weaknesses together with its successes.

At the present time, the PAIGC has reached the second phase mentioned above. The revolutionary army is growing, with the village militias as an auxiliary. More than half the country has been liberated and the villages are politically organized. The peasants produce more rice than they did during the colonial occupation and they are feeding the combatants, furnishing them with information, and giving them their sons. The Party—absorbed though it is in waging the war—has sent four times as many children to school as the Portuguese did. In the south, people's stores have met the elementary needs of the population for goods it could not produce itself.

The Portuguese ground forces hardly ever leave their garrisons in the liberated regions. Since the summer of 1966, the PAIGC has successfully undertaken the destruction of isolated posts, the stoppage of all river traffic, and the liberation of the central region of Boe so as to link the two regions already under its control, and it has at the same time politically indoctrinated the newly liberated populations and assured the economic stability of these zones.

The PAIGC appears to be within reach of the highest point of the second, developmental phase.[27] It has passed from harassment to offensive action and to the destruction of isolated posts —which presupposes a relatively substantial concentration of material means. Will the PAIGC succeed, during the coming years, in moving into the final phase, the all-out, destructive offensive? Guerrilla warfare is in effect a transitory form of warfare; its rule is harassment. But to pass on to the destructive offensive, the rebels must be capable of striking the enemy in a decisive way at some given point. The Portuguese remain for the moment superior in numbers and in armament.

In the past twenty-five years, only three guerrilla movements— the Chinese, the Vietnamese, and the Cuban—have succeeded in achieving such results. It should be added that whereas in the neo-colonial context it is necessary to crush the enemy totally, in the colonial context the war of national liberation can, as in Algeria, culminate in independence through negotiation. If Portugal found itself obliged to go to the conference table, the military situation created by the Guinean guerrillas would permit them to negotiate from a position of strength.

The PAIGC bears a very heavy burden. Its future successes as well as its failures (in the context of independence as well as in the context of the struggle) will be extremely instructive for Africa, insofar as it has until now been able, through its struggle and the social goals that inspire it, to capture the rank of vanguard.

May 1966–March 1967

---

[27] At this level the important program arises of linking the rural struggle with the various forms of urban struggle. This is a problem of prime importance.

Appendix

Portuguese Psychological Warfare Circulars

Circular No. 2
Our Cause Is Just

According to the terms of traditional military ethics, classical warfare involves two antagonists fighting against each other for the exclusive purpose of gaining command over disputed territory, and, by general agreement, the civilian population keeps away from the battlefield. Hence, war is conceived primarily as a struggle between two military opponents.

We are waging a different kind of war. First of all, this is a war for population control: whoever wins over the population will have the upper hand. We must remember what has happened in Guinea. The Province was leading a perfectly normal existence in a climate of peace and tranquillity—the only climate favorable to work, welfare, and wealth. Everything had perhaps not been completed to perfection, but the social climate was definitely a good one. For a long time, the I.N.[1] fighting us today in Angola and here in Guinea has been trying to persuade the peoples of Portuguese Africa that the Blacks can better their living conditions only if the Whites leave. In their opinion, this is the most effective and quickest way of improving the Africans' standard of living. "Throw the white man into the sea."

Then they started fighting again. From all appearances, they were supported by foreign powers who had designs on the Portuguese Provinces. These powers supplied them with arms and also trained their first guerrilla leaders. Thus, in Angola as in Guinea, we were driven into the war by a common enemy who

---

[1] *Inimigo:* enemy.

forced us to take arms in defense of our people and our heritage. The entire population did not immediately side with the enemy. Perhaps the vast majority would have preferred to have peace and to work in peace for a better future. But the enemy was not concerned with this: he terrorized and killed people, forcing them to flee and then to resettle in new forest zones where he can easily control them and put them to work for him. The I.N. thus created a more favorable situation for his resistance against our military efforts to re-establish peace and order. Here, as well as in Angola, we are all acquainted with specific cases that show how the I.N. keeps the population in check with terroristic methods. He has adopted this system of *conditioning* and adheres to it: those who do not obey him are either subjected to reprisals or killed outright. As everyone knows, the guerrilla cannot fight against an army like ours without the support of the population, which procures money and food for him, gives him information about us, and supplies him with the shelters and hiding places he needs. The guerrilla infiltrates reputedly peaceful villages; he abandons his weapon and hides it, only to reappear as a sympathizer and a friend, for he greets the troops warmly and attempts to render them services. Worse yet, since they know that because we are soldiers, we are inclined to consider as terrorists only the men who shoot at us in ambush and that we do not distrust women, old men, youngsters, etc., these are precisely the people whom the guerrillas use as liaison agents, informants, and supply-channels for rations, medicine, and ammunition.

This is the situation at present. What must we do? Given this state of affairs, how can we identify and define all those who are fighting against us? What should our objective be now? What shall our military ethics be vis-à-vis this I.N.? Can we continue to regard only those who shoot at us as the I.N.? When we capture a man out of uniform who does not fight us fairly but instead systematically attacks us from behind, must we treat him as a prisoner of war? Or should we rather consider him as an evildoer and a murderer who has been the cause of so much suffering? What is your opinion? We must control the population; we must force it to leave zones where the environment is favorable to guerrilla warfare; we must get it to settle in regions where we can guarantee protection and security. Those who do not want war must have an opportunity to find shelter. In this way, the guerrilla will become isolated: we will be able to recognize him, and he will no longer have the support he needs. Those who do not come with us and who refuse to execute our orders join forces with the I.N. who fights us from the forest. We must neutralize him, destroy him, kill him. That is our goal. Inefficiency, amateurishness, and irresponsibility have no place in our code of military ethics. If we fail to destroy the I.N.—if we fail to pursue this task with our deepest concern and our fullest effort—then we must bear responsibility for the death of all those who fall victim to the I.N. It is true that the population plays a crucial role in the political, economic, social, racial, and military aspects of this many-sided war, and that it devolves upon our Fatherland to settle all of these questions. However, it is also true that the army must settle the military problem. This is our principal concern at present. War is an evil, but we did not start this war. Now that it is underway, we must win victory. Defeat is always worse than victory—even in football! We did not come here for a two-year stint: we came to win the war. The army's job is to settle the military problem. This means that it will be necessary to kill. The army has assigned to its commandos the specific mission of killing in order to destroy the I.N. who fights us from the forest. Our mission consists in neutralizing the population and in destroying the I.N. so that the entire Portuguese world may live in peace and work for a better future.

OUR CAUSE IS JUST.

Circular No. 3
The Prisoner

When a soldier who fights under his army's colors and wears a uniform is taken prisoner, he is entitled to be respected as a soldier.

He is required to give only his name, his serial number, and the name of his unit.

The terrorist is not a soldier because when he is in combat he does not assume the risks inherent in wearing a uniform that identifies him as an enemy fighter. He runs away, hides, and blends in with the population. He is more a murderer than a soldier. According to traditional army ethics, a fighter captured out of uniform should be shot. But it is important to take prisoners. Only they can supply us with information, and this is why we do not shoot them, even though we have the right to do so, since they fight without uniforms.

The terrorist must be efficiently interrogated. They are not all equally capable of answering our questions about their organization; however, without exception, they must all inform us about their immediate superiors, their close friends, and their subordinates—as well as about the site of their activities. If we deal with them in this way we will succeed in discovering the hidden center of terrorist operations, and once we know its location, we will be able to destroy it.

If we fail to obtain this information from the terrorist, then we will be guilty of inefficiency and irresponsibility.

We must give him a chance to talk on his own initiative. If he does not do so, we will adopt more effective methods that will quickly convince him to collaborate with us. We will even go so far as to shoot him, as military ethics requires us to do in the case of every captured fighter who cannot prove the identity of his unit.

This is not a question of torture but of efficiency.

One risks one's life in combat. Don't give the I.N. a chance to beat you.

Wage war efficiently.

Note: Read this circular together with another soldier and exchange ideas about it with him.

"VOICE" No. 5
THE COMMANDO DOESN'T MISS

Each shot is one enemy less: the soldier's functions are to shoot and to kill.

The commandos are the most qualified combat troops of all. Their mission is to destroy the enemy who fights us from the forest.

You must be prepared to kill—not casually, for killing is a serious matter—but efficiently.

The commandos are not concerned with all aspects of this war. Our mission is to destroy and to kill.

This is why we are a special company.

We accomplish our mission efficiently.

Sometimes women and children are killed during our raids.

Note, however, that the enemy takes advantage of our moral sense and uses women and children directly or indirectly in combat.

The terrorist hides behind them. He takes shelter in the most peaceful looking huts of all.

If by chance innocent people should die, responsibility for their death belongs to the enemy and not to us.

THE COMMANDO KILLS EFFICIENTLY.

THE COMMANDO'S VOICE HAS SPOKEN.

Foreign Interests in "Portuguese" Guinea

The economy is concentrated in the hands of a few major Portuguese financial groups.

Some of the Portuguese enterprises active in Guinea are directly or indirectly affiliated with big non-Portuguese enterprises or with big international monopolies. This is strikingly demonstrated in parts of a report presented by the PAIGC at a seminar held in Cairo in October 1966, "National and Social Revolution in Africa," organized by the journals *Al Tallia* and the *Nouvelle Revue Internationale.*

Banco Nacional Ultramarino

As one of the major Portuguese monopolist banks, this bank exercises centralized control over all banking activity in Guinea.

In 1963, it succeeded in more than doubling its capital, from 200,000 contos[2] ($6,896,520) to 500,000 contos ($17,241,300). However, when this nominal capital is calculated by stock exchange quotations it amounts to more than 1,500,000 contos ($51,723,900). This bank has fifty-two branches in Portugal, with twenty more in the Portuguese colonies. Moreover, it has many branches abroad. Among its directors are some of the leading figures of Portuguese fascism and colonialism:

—Dr. Francisco Veiira Machado, President of the Board of Directors, former Colonial Secretary.

—Commandant Gabriel Teixeira, cabinet minister; former governor of Mozambique.

—Dr. Antonio Julio Castro Fernandes, member of the Fiscal Council, former Minister of Corporations.

—Dr. Pedro Theotonio Pereira, member of the Fiscal Council, former Secretary of State for the Presidency.

—Dr. Rafael Duque, member of the Fiscal Council, Commissioner representing the Portuguese government in the bank's board of directors, former Colonial Secretary.

Major shareholders in the BNU include representatives of some

---

[2] 1 conto = 1,000 escudos = $34.50 (approximately).

132

of Portugal's leading financial groups: Semmer, a big landowner associated with the Melo family of the Companhia União Fabril (CUF); Theatonio Pereira; Cohen; Alvaro de Brée, one of the directors of the famous Companhia dos Diamantes de Angola (DIAMANG), or Angola Diamond Company; Stau Monteiro; Inolstein Beck, Duke of Palmela; Pinto Basto; Soares de Albergaria; Monteiro Belard; Sousa Lara; etc.; also a number of big financiers such as D. Diogo Pessanha, Antonio Piano, and D. Artur Menezes Correia de Sa (Viscount de Merceana), who is also Vice-President of the bank.

Several important foreign banks are linked with the BNU; for example: the Crédit Franco-Portugais, the Comptoir National d'Escompte de Paris, the Midland Bank Executor and Trustee Company, the Westminster Bank Limited, and the Banco Hispano-Americano.

The BNU's gross and net profits mount steadily. The following figures illustrate its power and growth:

	GROSS PROFITS		NET PROFITS
Year	*Value* (*in contos*)	*Year*	*Value* (*in contos*)
1950	187,476	1956	67,547
1955	292,606	1957	73,517
1956	355,191	—	—
1957	360,089	1962	80,000
—	—	1963	85,000

In 1961, the figure for the fiscal year was given as 186,828 contos ($6,442,344).

In 1964, dividends were nine percent.

Among the BNU's closest business associations are the following: Metalúrgica Duarte Ferreira, Companhia Agrícola-Pecuária de Angola (stock-farming and agriculture), Companhia de Seguros a Mundial (insurance), Companhia Geral de Angola (agricultural, industrial, and commercial activities, fisheries, soap and oil production), Sociedade Lino e Couto, Amoníaco Português (nitrates), SONEFE (investments, research and development), Pinto de Magalhães Limitada (bank), Banco da Agricultura, Banco Raposo de Magalhães, Banco Português do Atlântico, Banco Borges & Irmão, Banco Lisboa e Açores, Anglo-Portuguese Bank, Banque Franco-Portugaise d'Outre-Mer, Banco Ultramarino Brasileiro, Westminster Bank Limited, Banco Hispano-Americano, Comptoire National d'Escompte de Paris, Banco F. Alves Pinto Leite, Sociedade Comercial Ultramarina, Companhia de Moçambique (agriculture and stock-farming), Petrofina (petroleum), Alumínio Portugues de Angola-Péchiney (aluminum industry).

The BNU is bank of issue for all the Portuguese colonies except Angola and has vested interests in such Angolan firms as the Companhia Geral de Angola (General Company of Angola), and the Companhia Agrícola-Pecuaria de Angola (Company for Agriculture and Stockbreeding of Angola).

It is moreover tied to the Angolan economy by links with various giant enterprises, such as SONEFE, and by its participation in the banking interests of the big Sousa Lara financial family (proprietors of the all-powerful Companhia do Açucar de Angola, or Angola Sugar Company).

The Companhia de Moçambique owns shares in the BNU, but it is more importantly the major shareholder in the following enterprises: Companhia Colonial do Buzi (13,131 shares), the Trans-Zambezia Railway (200,000 shares), Companhia do Porto da Beira (120,000 shares), Companhia dos Diamantes de Angola (DIAMANG) (5,000 shares), União Electrica Portuguesa (1,210 shares), the Nyasaland Railways (3,733 shares), the Beira Railways (9,200 shares).

Principal shareholder in Alumínio Portugues de Angola (Portuguese Aluminum of Angola) is the French trust of Péchiney, Compagnie des Produits Chimiques et électro-métallurgiques (Chemical and Electro-metallurgical Products Company), which owns all series B shares in this enterprise (2,000 shares).

Companhia União Fabril (CUF)

A giant among Portuguese industries, the CUF was founded at the turn of the century, starting with agriculture and moving on to textiles, copper, sulfates, sulfuric acid, steel, ship construction, etc. The CUF has become one of the biggest monopolies in the Iberian peninsula and a great power among European enterprises. It employs tens of thousands of laborers in the firms under its aegis. It owns a private merchant fleet, whole industries, etc. The CUF belongs to the Melo family, which is linked in turn by marriage to one of Portugal's biggest finance groups, the Champalimaud family, which has a near monopoly on the Portuguese steel industry, itself largely under West German control.

The CUF has joint interests with various West German, French, and U.S. firms.

In 1957, its capital totalled 4,800,000 contos (about $170 million).

In 1962, the CUF signed a contract with the Société Française d'Etudes et de Financements Industriels whereby it would supply raw materials for the installation and construction of new plants, some of them in Guinea, especially for the chemical and textile branches of the enterprise. The contract involved seventy-seven million New Francs (462,000 contos).

The CUF received, during the first months of 1963, credits amounting to 120,000 contos (about $420,000) from France and West Germany. It took this occasion to form a new company in conjunction with the big American firm, the Ludlow Corporation: Sociedade de Industrias Texteis do Norte—SETENOR (Textile Industries Corporation of the North).

A jute-processing plant was set up at Matosinhos, in northern Portugal, in which the CUF invested 80,000 contos ($275,862).

In Guinea, Americo Sotto Maior held a controlling interest in NOSOCO, a corporation affiliated with UNILEVER, which is entrenched in both Senegal and "Portuguese" Guinea. From 1961 on, NOSOCO stopped its commercial activities in Guinea and has been represented there by a holding company, with which the other firms made working arrangements and settled accounts concerning the firm. Certain former NOSOCO representations then passed into the hands of Sotto Maior, as in the case of Shell, Philips, certain electrical manufacturers, etc. . . .

Petrofina

Petrofina is linked with SACOR and the BNU, both giant enterprises which together play a disproportionately important role in the economic life of the country.

Petrofina is linked with several Portuguese colonial enterprises which by themselves constitute great economic powers if not authentic monopolies, such as the Bank of Angola.

SACOR (*Sociedade Anónima Concessionária de Refinação de petróleos*)

This firm has the monopoly of oil refining in Portugal.

SACOR was founded in 1938, with an original capital of 15,000 contos ($517,240). In 1962 its nominal capital totalled 496,000 contos (in other words, it is now thirty-three times larger than it was at the start).

In 1959 SACOR made a gross profit of 352,000 contos (about $11,900,000) and a net profit of 128,000 contos (about $4,400,000). Its 1962 profits totalled roughly 240,000 contos.

The Chairman of the Board of Directors is Professor Costa Leite (Combrales), a former Salazar cabinet minister and head of the Legião Portuguesa (fascist militia).

"In Guinea, SACOR has set up new oil storage facilities. These facilities are located at Bandim (Bissau) and cover a surface of 20,000 square meters."—*Industria Portuguesa*, No. 432 (February 1964), p. 92. Their cost was 18,000 contos.

Other Firms Operating in Guinea

BIG CORPORATIONS

Antonio Silva corporation

This enterprise is affiliated with the Companhia União Fabril (CUF) which has the monopoly of commercial activity in "Portuguese" Guinea. As we have already shown, this is the oldest, most solid, and most strongly rooted Portuguese firm in Guinea. Its investments in the country total several tens of thousands of contos. It has its own merchant fleet. Its commercial activities include an import-export business, industry, shipping, and insurance.

Sociedade Comercial Ultramarina
(Overseas Commercial Corporation)

This house ranks second in the export-import business. Its activities extend to certain portions of the interior in Guinea. It possesses, aside from warehouses, modern rice-threshing plants, as well as oil-extraction and soap factories.

The company president in 1958 was D. Luis Pereira Coutinho, a financier belonging to the Portuguese aristocracy and representing the Banco Nacional Ultramarino (BNU).

According to the BNU's quarterly bulletin of March 1958, the corporation owns an industrial complex in the industrial section of Bissau, with individual plants for rice and peanut hulling and for the extraction of vegetable oils. Investment totalled roughly 20,000 contos ($682,758).

Companhia Lusitana do Alumínio
da Guiné e Angola

This corporation's objective is the discovery and processing of bauxites. It was founded on August 16, 1957, by the terms of a contract signed on March 7, 1957, between the Portuguese government and the Dutch firm Billiton Maatschappij N.V.

It has a capital of 5,000 contos ($172,413).

Esso Exploration Guinea, Inc.

Founded in 1958, it has a capital of 43,500 contos. Although the main offices are in Wilmington, Delaware, its biggest office is located in Bissau.

It is affiliated with Standard Oil of New Jersey and its agent, the Corporation Trust Company of America. (Standard Oil is the biggest American oil company after Gulf, and belongs to the group of the eight biggest oil companies in the world.)

In March 1958, Esso made a new contract with the colony of Guinea, whereby it obtained a concession comprising 50,000 square kilometers, in other words the total area of the country including its underwater territory.

In accordance with the terms of this new contract, the Portuguese government gives Esso a concession including "the right to prospect and exploit for its own benefit for forty-five years dating from the signature of the contract the installations existing in the area which it wishes to retain."

Furthermore, the Portuguese government gives it every facility "for the construction of industrial buildings and installations, as well as commercial, social, or housing facilities, including roads, telephone and electric power lines, radio transmitting and receiving stations, airports, wharfs, docks, and breakwaters . . . ," and exempts the corporation from taxes and duties on either its business activities or on its importation of materials, equipment, and other supplies. The corporation is even authorized to export any substance extracted in the concession area with the same tax and duty exemptions.

In accordance with the terms of the contract, "the colonial government will seek to facilitate the concession of the foreign exchange stock necessary to the corporation's activities."

In the complementary contract signed between the colony of Guinea, Standard Oil of New Jersey, and Esso in March 1966, Esso "may also undertake prospecting, drilling, and exploitation of any other mineral."

Thanks to these kinds of concessions, the Portuguese government presumes that it can manipulate the possibility of a more direct intervention of its allies in the colonial war, in view of the increasing difficulties it encounters in maintaining its presence in the countryside and of the growing success of our national liberation struggle and the enlargement of our liberated regions.

Companhia da Borracha da Guine, CABORNEL (*Guinea Rubber Company*)

Its aim is the exploitation of Guinea's rubber resources. It owns factories whose operations began toward the end of 1957, furnishing raw material for FABOPOL—Fábrica Portuguesa de Borracha, (a factory operating in Porto)—upon which CABORNEL is dependent.

ENTERPRISES OF MEDIUM SIZE

Sociedade de Fomento Agricole e Industrial da Guine, (SOFAIGUI) (Agricultural and Industrial Development Corporation of Guinea).

Sociedade de Investimentos da Guine.

Companhia Agrícola e Fabril da Guine (AGRIFA) (Agricultural and Industrial Company of Guinea).

Sociedade Algodoeira da Guine (Cotton Corporation of Guinea). This corporation had as its president Rafael Duque, who was Colonial Secretary and Commissioner representing the Portuguese government in the Overseas National Bank's (BNU) board of directors.

SMALLER ENTERPRISES

Virgílio Agostinho Júnior: wholesale business and representation of foreign firms for various products.

Costa Campos Limitade: wholesale business and representation.

Sociedade Madeireira da Guine—SOMAGUI (Guinea Lumber Corporation); *Guiné Industrial de Madeiras* (lumbering); *Empresa de Madeiras Africana* (Africa Lumber Enterprise).

Sociedade Commercial de Representaçoes (Commercial Representation Corporation): wholesale commerce, pharmaceutical products, and representation for Portuguese and foreign firms.

Construções Limitade: sale of construction materials; agent for various firms.

J. da Costa Pinheiro: wholesale commerce; agent for numerous foreign firms.

Gouveia e Companhia Limitada.

Sociedade Frigorífica Exportadora Limitada (Export Refrigeration Corporation).

Bibliography

Basic works

James Duffy, *Portugal in Africa*. London: 1960.
Texeira da Mota, *Guinea Portuguesa*. Lisbon: Agencia Geral do Ultramar, 1954. 2 vols.

General works

Perry Anderson, *Le Portugal et la fin de l'ultracolonialisme*. Paris: François Maspero, 1963.
Amilcar Cabral, *Rapport aux Nations-Unis*. PAIGC: 1962.

Pamphlets and papers

Amilcar Cabral, "Guinée, Cap Vert face au colonialisme portugais," *Partisans* No. 7 (1962).
——, "L'arme de la théorie," *Partisans*, Nos. 26–27 (1966).
——, "La lutte en Guinée," *Revue Internationale du Socialisme*, No. 4 (1964).
Gérard Chaliand, *Guinée portugaise et Cap Vert en lutte pour leur indépendance*. Paris: F. Maspero, 1964.
D. A. Faber and J. Mettas, "Guinée 'portugaise' 1962," *Les Temps Modernes*, No. 198, November 1962.
Alfredo Margarido, "Les partis politiques en Guinée portugaise, en Angola, et aux îles du Cap Vert," *Le mois en Afrique*, No. 9 (1966).
Jean Mettas, "La guerre de Guinée," *Aletheia*, No. 3 (1964).

Articles from the French press

G. Chaliand, *Le Nouvel Observateur*, No. 87, July 1966.
M. Honorin, *Croissance des Jeunes Nations*, No. 60, November 1966.

141

L'Humanité-Dimanche, No. 78, August 1966 (interview with M. Marret and I. Romero).

J. Vieyra, *Jeune Afrique*, No. 290, July 1966.

Documentary films

Lala quema, by Mario Marret, 1964 (banned in France, 1965).

Lavante negro, by P. Nelli, cameraman, E. Bentivoglio, 1966 (prize at the Venice Biennale).

Nossa terra, by Mario Marret, assisted by Isidro Romero, 1966.

Note: Documentaries were also made by a team from the German Democratic Republic in 1964, by Dutch television reporters in 1966, by M. Honorin and P. Dumez for the ORTF *Panorama* in 1966, and by the Italian V. Orsini, in 1967.